ENLISTED
and
ALONE

Memoir of a Navy SEAL Wife

Cindy Messer

Enlisted and Alone
Memoir of a Navy SEAL Wife

Cynthia D. Messer,
4 Boys Press, LLC
PO Box 6632
Virginia Beach, VA 23456
www.enlistedandalone.com

Enlisted and Alone, Cindy Messer — 1st ed.
ISBN 978-0-9997342-0-9

Dedicated to:
My husband Steve and our boys
Military wives and their families
Every wife who feels alone in a marriage
Survivors of suicide
My family and friends who have shared this journey

PREFACE

"Life has got to be lived, that's all there is to it."
—ELEANOR ROOSEVELT

IT HAS BEEN TWELVE YEARS since my husband Steve retired from the Navy Sea, Air, and Land (SEAL) Teams. He proudly served twenty-two years. Most of the nineteen years he spent as an active duty SEAL operator in the "Teams" were as a sniper and Joint Terminal Attack Controller (JTAC). Since his retirement we have moved several times, always looking for the dream home and the next big project as an entrepreneur, contractor, or tactical training expert for some branch of the government.

This has ranged from tree removal, installing irrigation and outdoor lighting, to SWAT and Special Operations training instructor, to a FAA licensed drone pilot. Always chasing the American dream. During this chase, I was in the background raising our boys and taking care of our home — alone much of the time.

I didn't realize I was slowly losing my self-worth and identity.

Hanging onto this ride has been a challenge.

Now, some 14 years later, we're back in Virginia Beach, the only place that really feels like home to us.

We even live in the same zip code where we purchased our first house and brought our baby boys home to.

I call this last move our "Full Circle."

Steve had a difficult time navigating the "real world" when he left the Teams without his tight-knit family of frogmen surrounding him any longer. Work ethics, loyalty, sense of purpose, it all was different.

He found the lifestyle of working what he called a "J-O-B" left him frustrated and feeling empty. He missed the guys he worked with, the mission, the camaraderie, and the adrenalin.

I believe most SEALS go through this phase, experiencing feelings of guilt and a sense of having made a mistake by retiring or leaving the community. As his wife, I kept praying and hoping he would find his way and discover the right thing and the right people he enjoyed working with.

It was difficult—there was nothing I could do to help him.

Eventually, he found where he belongs, but it took years.

As a wife, I knew my support was very important during both the good and the bad times. I focused on our two boys and what I felt they deserved and needed, and that's what kept me motivated to stay in our relationship and move forward. I didn't want my boys to grow up without their dad, especially after he retired from a career he loved to spend more time at home and really get to know them.

Nor did I want them to be torn between the two of us, or to have to meet and be a part of another man's life and family.

It's not what I wanted for them, or for us as a family.

I loved him and our boys, and even though the road was long and hard, we had to keep moving forward together.

Since moving back to Virginia Beach in 2015, we've sadly attended two memorial services for SEALs killed in combat within months of each other. Recently, I sat next to Steve in a packed movie theater on base, surrounded by handsome men wearing Navy dress blue uniforms, with chests of ribbons and large gold Tridents.

There were young, middle-aged, and gray-haired SEALs, all present to honor the family and their young warrior, his casket now draped by the United States Flag at the front of the theater.

I studied the wooden cross behind the casket with those familiar tan boots, rifle, chest gear, fins, and combat helmet with night vision goggles.

I thought to myself, *those same tan boots have walked through our door for years.*

This could have been us.

The wife and her small children here today could have been me and our boys just like her. I had a slight panic attack as the service began, *what right do I have, to write a book about being the wife of a SEAL?*

Look at this poor woman and her children, her life has forever changed, and now her children will grow up without their dad.

Why did this have to happen to this family?

My heart ached for the SEAL's mother sitting next to his young wife. She'll never see or touch her son again. I just couldn't imagine the pain of the loss of a child.

How do you get past this?

How do you go on?

I don't have the answers, but I have been a widow, even though my husband was not killed in combat. I believe the loss and the pain is the same when you lose your spouse, no matter how they leave this earth.

~

After the memorial, we navigated through teammates, other service members, friends and family, and as I sat down in our car I thought, *all there is in the end is memories for those left behind.*

This warrior was so young, but after listening to his devastated wife, teammates, and friends honor him, he left them with many great stories and memories they'll carry for the rest of their lives.

Thank God, they have those to cherish and hold onto forever.

I hope when my time is up, my boys will think of me and remember how very much I loved them, and know I would have done anything on the face of the earth to protect them.

I did my very best to raise them alone when their dad was away protecting our country. I know I made mistakes, but I navigated through parenthood to the best of my ability and I loved their dad through it all.

We didn't personally know either of these fine young men, but, because of who they are and who we are, we're all SEAL family.

As teammates and family, we always go to pay our respects, celebrate their lives, and honor their loved ones in humble gratitude for the way they protect each other, our country, and our way of life.

The service and the gathering of Brothers, family, and teammates instills an incredible sense of pride for the SEAL community and the United States military.

Through the tears, I instantly knew I was indeed in the company of warriors, family, friends, and true American heroes.

If you grew up in a military family, served on active duty, or married into the military, you may have experienced something similar and understand what it feels like to attend one of these memorials.

As I always have, I left feeling emotionally exhausted and very sad for this family, as I do for every family that loses a loved one.

In an instant, all you know and love can be gone forever.

Every time I hear Keith Urban sing "For You" on the radio, I find myself listening closely to the words as tears roll down my cheeks. I can't help but think about all the guys that can relate to that song and the hurt for the ones that lost their lives protecting their Brothers.

Team Guys won't hesitate to put their life on the line for each other. It's hard to imagine that kind of commitment, but as a mother I can relate in a way, as I know I wouldn't hesitate to step in front of a bullet for one of my boys, not even a millisecond.

Everyone's life story is different. By sharing mine, I hope to inspire others and give hope.

Not many things are easy in this life, but you're stronger than you think you are. I learned to navigate situations in our marriage I didn't even know existed, and somehow, I managed to climb over each obstacle, gaining strength I never knew I had.

My plate was so full, but the loneliness was the hardest. I'm not sure you ever learn how to deal with that, it is what it is.

No matter how strong you think you are, the loneliness creeps into your soul and leaves a sad empty feeling. Each of us deals with this differently in our own way, and right or wrong, we all struggle with it.

I hope the experiences I've had and the trials I've endured help another military wife navigate through difficult times, help her stay focused on her family and know she's not alone.

I hope by reading my book, she'll find strength and a sense of encouragement to fight the good fight, stay with her husband, and not throw in the towel when times get tough.

"The storms in our lives may be difficult, but as each challenge passes, we learn that we have within us the strength and ability to keep on going..."
–HEATHER A. STILLUFSEN

CONTENTS

CHAPTER 1

MY STORY

"Not all of us can do great things. But we can do small things with great love."

—MOTHER TERESA

IN TIMES OF WAR AND PEACE, military wives often experience loss, heartbreak, divorce, loneliness, spouses returning home with PTSD or serious injuries, alcoholism, infidelity, and more.

I'm one of the fortunate ones that didn't lose my husband to combat, a training accident, or divorce.

Like almost all SEALs, a long career in the Teams has taken its toll on Steve's body in many ways. He lives with his disabilities and has learned to adapt and deal with chronic pains, doing what he can physically, and working around his limitations.

We consider ourselves lucky to have our health and each other, and we fully appreciate the sacrifice of Steve's teammates and the many other conventional and Special Operations warriors who gave their lives, limbs, or eyesight in service to our nation.

We military wives all have our own stories, each unique and special in its own way. I share mine in hopes of helping other military wives to see that you're not alone, and that there are many military couples who successfully fight through the tough times, long deployments, loneliness, and countless other struggles that are a normal part of military life.

Marriage can last, love can grow, and families can remain together. It's not easy but it can be done.

2017 marks twenty-seven years together for Steve and I, with fifteen of those years for me as an active duty SEAL wife.

It's my hope that sharing my story may serve as an inspiration or helpful guide for military wives that may feel alone, frustrated, or afraid.

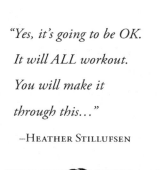

"Yes, it's going to be OK. It will ALL workout. You will make it through this…"

—HEATHER STILLUFSEN

I remember lying in bed one night next to our Black Lab Moose, crying from exhaustion during a long deployment period, thinking, *I didn't get married and have children to be alone and do this all by myself.*

My husband was gone, I had no idea where he was, no idea when he would be home, no cell phone, no email, no family for thousands of miles, and two boys at four and six years old, both sick with the flu.

Fevers, vomiting, diarrhea, constant changing of bed sheets, trips to the doctor, with nobody to call for a helping hand. With no end in sight, I had never felt so helpless and weak as I did that night.

Looking back, I realize I was so exhausted and worn down that I really felt I couldn't make it through another day.

But then morning came, and somehow I managed to keep going, day after day, week after week, month after month.

~

Moose was my best friend, confidant, protector, and playmate to our boys. I would lay in bed, hug him, and talk to him like he was a person, and at times I felt he understood what I was feeling and saying.

He looked after the boys, went on walks with us, relocated, and adapted to the many homes we lived in throughout Steve's career. I counted on him and he was always there through thick and thin.

When our family lost him to brain cancer at just ten years old, I lost my best friend, as did the boys and Steve too.

Steve has always said, "Taking Moose to the vet that snowy night in Idaho was the hardest thing I've ever had to do."

He was wrecked emotionally for several days.

Moose was so much more than just a pet, he was part of the family unit, almost human, almost like a child.

It was devastating to all of us.

We always seemed to have small backyards during Moose's early years. We would often joke around with him, talking to him as if he were human like we did every day, and tell him that Black Labs should have room to run, roam, and hunt.

Kind of making a promise in a way, we'd tell him we were going to get a place with five acres one day.

Well, we kept that promise and bought that nice "Five Acres" we had always talked about.

Located near Coeur d'Alene, Idaho, it was beautiful country, "God's Country," as Steve called it.

When Moose died, Steve wrapped him in his old camouflage Navy uniform coat, complete with all nametags and SEAL insignia, covered his head with a jungle flop hat so dirt wouldn't get in his eyes, and buried him under a large spruce tree.

His grave is marked by a hand carved stone Steve made for him, and I'm quite sure Moose is happy being so close to the quail, grouse, deer, elk, and other wildlife that roamed our property.

"A dog will teach you unconditional love. If you can have that in your life, things won't be too bad."
—Robert Wagner

A major consistency in the SEAL Team lifestyle is absence of your husband—he's never around.

The nature of Naval Special Warfare requires each operator to be an expert in at least one or more primary skillsets or specialties, and very well cross-trained in many others.

Reaching a high level of expertise spans many years of first-hand experience, and requires much professional development, education, and specialized training.

Unfortunately, the intensive pre-deployment schedule of constant squadron and small unit training for combat takes place mostly away from home base.

It always seemed to be a vicious cycle of schools and training, followed by workups, rehearsals, and exercises, culminating in a very long ninety-day to six-month or longer deployment.

You may wonder how I know this military lingo — well, I lived it for fifteen years, hearing it over and over when I would ask him why he had to leave again. It's like learning a new language.

Every homecoming was followed by a bittersweet reunion and a too-short leave period, only to start the whole cycle over again.

If he wasn't on deployment, he was gone somewhere…and he was gone consistently.

SEALs are very independent outside of their work environment. Like a good SEAL wife, or so I thought, I never wanted to bother anyone or ask for help. I thought I had to be strong and do everything by myself.

You know, mow the lawn while your toddler plays in the sandbox or your baby is in a pack on your back while you rake leaves and trim the hedges.

Or go to the grocery store with your toddler in the cart and the baby in the car seat in the cart with no room for groceries. Back then stores didn't have the large, car-style grocery carts for kids that they have now.

I'm sure my boys would have loved them, and maybe then grocery shopping would not have been one of those chores I put off until the very last minute possible.

Even taking a shower was a challenge, requiring timing or control.

Either both boys had to be sleeping, or both restrained, one in the bouncy swing hanging from the door frame, and one strapped down in the infant seat on the bathroom floor where I could peek out of the shower curtain every few minutes to see that they were okay.

From the time he was brought into this world by way of emergency C-section, our oldest son Nate was almost always up and awake throughout the night until he was three years old. When our youngest son Luke was born (also to C-section), not only was I up every two or three hours to breast feed him, but I was also up with Nate throughout the night.

I remember telling my neighbor, "I'm not going to remember much of this period in their lives because I feel like a walking zombie."

I literally had to tell myself each day, *I have to do this for my boys just to get through another day.*

The days would roll into weeks and months without Steve, and once again, little or no communication. I'd watch the news and try to figure out where he might be according to what was going on in the world at the time. I remember when President George Bush, Sr. had to step down, I sat and cried watching the TV. I felt he and Barbara were like grandparents looking out for our country and Steve.

Thanks to modern technology, today's military wives have so much more support and means of communication to help stay in touch, get help when they need it, and to generally feel less alone.

While it's common today to get on a Skype or Facetime call, send a text, or answer a phone call from across the world, that technology didn't exist for most people not long ago.

Yes, you read that right, no cell phone for many of those years. I remember how excited I was to get email when the internet came about, and would look many times each day to see if I had an email from Steve.

On one of his last deployments in 2003, I had the mailing address of a ship he was staging from, so I could send letters and boxes of goodies, which I did daily, even if it was just a letter.

I knew he only came back to the ship occasionally, but I was excited just to be able to write to him and let him know what was going on at home.

I finally felt a sense of communication from so far away, and I was so excited to be able to write my feelings to him and feel like we were connected in some way.

I've been to several social gatherings for SEAL wives in the last couple of years and am very impressed by the improvement of communication and support, not just for the wives, but families in general.

This is an important initiative for many reasons, even for a purpose that may seem trivial — like a social event for wives. Being home alone, raising kids and running a household without regular adult contact every day for months on end takes an emotional and mental toll.

The opportunity to get out of the house and spend time with friends and people that have something in common with each other helps adult women feel like adults again.

When the boys were little, I spent so much time around them and so little time socializing with adults, I felt at times like I couldn't communicate with an adult without speaking in baby talk.

Sounds crazy I know, but it happens.

Baseball, soccer and Taekwondo. I made sure that any sport the boys wanted to play, they did. And somehow, I would do all the running around to get them to practice and games.

I had to go into the sport knowing Steve would most likely be gone and I'd need to manage this alone.

I remember being the team mom of one of the baseball teams, and the parents were shocked to learn that I was married, and yes, the boys did have a living dad.

Unfortunately, he missed much of the younger childhood years of both boys. I believe this realization and the associated guilt of not seeing that first great hit at baseball, scoring a goal at a soccer game, or earning a new belt color at Taekwondo, later influenced him to leave his beloved Brothers in the Teams and move on to become a full time Dad at home.

I was fortunate that a couple of Steve's younger and single buddies would spend time with the boys when they could. They all knew they had a place at our table during the holidays, or anytime they wanted to bring their girlfriends over.

The first movie the boys watched about Navy SEALs was seen with one of the young guys from Steve's team. He came and picked us up, took us to the movie, and answered questions the boys had about it afterwards.

He tutored Nate with his math work, making it fun and able for him to understand.

This was a Godsend to me, as math was never one of my strong subjects. He also took the time to attend several Taekwondo classes to cheer the boys on.

To this day at ages twenty-five and twenty-two, Nate and Luke don't know his real name, but they certainly remember him by his nickname.

Occasionally, one of the guys would come over with his girlfriend to babysit for us so we could enjoy a night out when Steve was home. At Christmas time, I would find G.I. Joes hidden in our decorated tree, not hidden by my boys, but by these young Team Guys.

They were like sons to Steve and me both. I loved learning about them.

Where were they from?

What made them decide to go into the Teams?

They all had a different story, a different family life, a different reason they volunteered to become a SEAL over anything else they possibly could've done.

What was interesting to me was that at least half of the enlisted guys had college degrees, and they were extremely intelligent and talented in many ways.

Yet, with so many paths they could have taken to a high salary and successful career in the corporate world, they chose to join this elite warrior fraternity.

Today it fills my heart with happiness that our grown sons still stay in contact with two of the retired SEALs that many years ago were young SEAL operators that served under and alongside Steve on active duty.

They remain today in the boy's lives as trusted mentors and friends to both, only a text message or phone call away.

Every time Nate or Luke has reached out for advice or a friend to lean on, they stopped what they were doing and answered the call.

That's one of the cool things about SEALs; the guys grow up in an elite military unit, living, training, working, and deploying into harm's way together. They truly are friends and extended family for life.

It's neat to see how they react to one another after not seeing each other for sometimes years at a time. It's like they were never apart, and they pick up right where they left off. The guys that are close to Steve know he's there for them 24/7 should they ever need him, and he knows the ones that he could call on as well.

Unfortunately, following 9/11, these Brothers-in-Arms were reunited more often for memorial services than reunions.

Several young SEALs we welcomed into our home and hearts over the years made the ultimate sacrifice in combat. Some never had the chance to have children, get married, raise their kids, or grow old with the one they loved.

To this day Steve has photos of these "sons" of his on the wall in his office and they'll never be forgotten by our family.

I've never witnessed a family like the Brotherhood of the SEALs, these guys are truly like brothers.

I remember going to the annual reunion as the younger ones, and looking at the older Frogmen and their families thinking, *are we going to be them someday?*

Yes, we're now those elders, and the friendships last forever.

Steve has told me that from day one, "When the 'tadpoles' class up as a Basic Underwater Demolition/SEAL (BUDS) training class, the few that graduate together will likely never forget each other, especially if they serve on the same Teams and deploy together over the course of a career."

Many people live their whole life and never have a relationship with someone like many of these guys do.

I always thought when Steve said, "Brotherhood," it was kind of dorky.

I didn't understand it for many years, but I do now, and it is a brotherhood like no other.

How I became part of the SEAL community had to be God's plan, because after the death of my first husband, never in my wildest imagination could I have painted this canvas.

CHAPTER 2

SURVIVOR

"I wanted a perfect ending. Now I've learned, the hard way, that some poems don't rhyme, and some stories don't have a clear beginning, middle and end. Life is about not knowing, having to change, taking the moment and making the best of it without knowing what's going to happen next."
—GILDA RADNER

IT WAS A NORMAL SUNNY SPRING DAY in Mishawaka, Indiana, on May 28, 1986, when I drove into the driveway and pushed the garage door opener button like I did so many other days. When the garage door began to open, I immediately saw green fluid dripping from the bottom of the door.

I wondered what the liquid was as the door began to open and I saw my husband's company car backed into the garage, the floor flooded with the green fluid.

Even today, I still remember being puzzled about the puddle as the door continued upward on its track.

As it opened all the way, I saw my first husband Brian, sitting in the driver seat with his head back on the head rest staring at me with his mouth open.

I sat in my car and looked at him for a moment and wondered, *what is he doing?*

I got out of my car, walked into the narrow space between the car and the wall, and looked at him through the closed driver side window. He had backed the car into the garage close to the wall where the driver's door was unable to be opened all the way.

I felt an instant bolt of panic run through my body as I knew something horrible had just happened. I instinctively leaped into action to try and save him.

I ran around to the passenger side, yanked the door open and jumped inside, climbing across the passenger seat in my work dress. I shook him and saw his beautiful blue eyes glazed over and still. His mouth was open, and his tongue was swollen.

He was not a small guy and I have no idea to this day how I did it, but somehow, unbelievable strength came over me as I pulled him across the seat and out onto the garage floor.

The smell of engine exhaust, melted rubber, plastic, and hot motor parts burned my eyes and I felt like I couldn't get any fresh air into my lungs.

The exhaust fumes were choking and overpowering.

I ran to the driveway looking for someone, anyone, as I screamed, "Help! Someone help me!" and ran back into the garage, dropping down to start CPR on his lifeless body.

A construction worker down the street saw the commotion, ran up the street into the garage, and saw me desperately trying to save him. He pulled me off Brian and began CPR.

My neighbor ran into the driveway, saw what was happening, and ran back into her house to call an ambulance on the landline.

We had never even heard of such a concept as cell phones back then.

The panic hit me hard as I began to cry and ask the construction worker repeatedly if Brian was going to be okay. He just had to be, this wasn't real, right?

I still hadn't realized what had really happened to Brian.

The ambulance arrived, and I remember telling them they had to save him, that he couldn't die.

They loaded him onto the stretcher, placing a mask on his face as one of the EMTs began pumping something in his hand.

I told them I had to go with them and they made me get in the front seat. The ride to the hospital seemed to take forever.

I looked down at my feet and realized I had no shoes on and my nylons were shredded up to my ankles exposing my bare feet. I kept looking back through the partition window, not seeing Brian, but only the backs of the EMTs working on him. I remember asking the driver if he could please drive faster, and telling him that nothing could happen to Brian.

I found out later Brian had been dead for several hours before I found him.

Did the construction worker know, and that's why he pulled me away and took over?

Did the EMT's know but they continued to work on him anyway?

Did everyone know but me?

I was obviously in shock and refused to even let my mind go there. I was taken to a room once we arrived at the hospital, and sat there alone in my bare feet, no purse, just the clothes on my back, waiting for someone to tell me what had happened and that he would be okay.

A minister eventually entered the room as I wondered to myself, *why is he here?*

I need to see the doctor, not a minister.

He came over to me and handed me Brian's wallet, wedding ring and watch, and proceeded to tell me Brian had committed suicide and he was dead.

Suicide?

There is no way in hell the Brian I had known for the last six years would do such a thing.

I stared at his things and thought, *this has to be a horrible nightmare, there's no way it can really be happening.*

I asked if I could use the phone and he told me yes, but the call must be a collect call.

Yeah, collect.

No free long distance.

Somebody had to pay for it.

I remember dialing my parent's phone number in Memphis, needing to talk to my dad and hear him tell me this didn't happen, and that everything would be ok.

My mom accepted my collect call and I said, "Mom, Brian is dead, he's committed suicide."

She dropped the phone, screaming something I don't remember, and at that point I knew it wasn't a bad dream.

This wasn't just a horrible nightmare, and I wasn't going to wake up in a cold sweat, glad that it wasn't real.

I stood in the room alone and thought, *what do I do now?*
I had no idea.

I don't remember why, but I didn't get to see Brian at the hospital. I didn't see him again until I saw him at the funeral home.

Do I go back home?

I didn't want to leave him here alone.

Where will he go?

Where do they take him?

Why did he leave me?

I felt the hot tears running down my face and my heart was pounding. My legs were weak, and I felt like I was going to get sick.

There was a knock at the door and a doctor in a white lab coat came in and told me that he had died from extreme carbon monoxide poisoning.

He told me Brian was an organ donor according to his driver's license, but only his eye corneas could be used for donation due to his organs being so badly damaged. He also told me I was lucky that I hadn't been overcome by the carbon monoxide fumes as well, considering the extremely high CO levels in his blood.

After getting myself together so I could speak, I called my neighbor Sharon and asked her if she could come pick me up from the hospital, that Brian had died.

She and her husband came, held me in their arms for a bit, then put me in the car. After I had left with the ambulance, the neighbors closed my car door, went into the house, got our little dog Bobbie-Jo out, and closed the garage door.

As we pulled into their driveway, I got out of the car and without thinking, started walking towards our house. Sharon grabbed me and told me I shouldn't go home, but to come inside with them.

Once inside, I was greeted by our sweet little adopted Bobbie-Jo.

Did she know?

Could she sense what had just happened in the garage only hours earlier?

Brian had put her in the house and closed the utility room door and the door leading to the garage. It's my guess he was trying to protect her from the fumes.

I spent the rest of night awake in their guest bedroom in my dress and bare feet, looking out the window at our house, holding Bobbie-Jo as I waited for my mom and dad to arrive. *Did someone call his parents?*

Oh my God, I thought, *this is going to kill his mom and dad, and his whole family.*

I had no idea who had contacted whomever, I just knew I needed my family to come and help me, like right away.

Once Mom arrived, we went into the house. A friend of our family had picked her up at the airport and drove her to our house. He was kind enough to have the car removed from our garage.

The car's engine had been revved at high rpm for so long that the engine had overheated to the point of blowing a radiator hose and self-destructed from loss of coolant.

There were melted plastic and rubber parts on the engine, bits and pieces of melted parts on the garage floor, just an awful, stinking mess.

I found out later that the green liquid all over the garage floor was radiator fluid.

My mind was racing with uncontrollable thoughts about how long it took him to die.

Or what if he had changed his mind at the last minute, but was immobilized, unable to stop the deadly chain of events he set in motion?

I had just spoken to him on the phone at noon, we were going to go to the gym we recently joined, and he told me he loved me as he did every day.

What had happened to make him do this?

The phone rang and before anyone could answer, our answering machine picked up the call and I heard Brian's voice on the recorder.

I remember falling to my knees, *this could not be real.*

Dad didn't come with Mom right away.

I remember crying and telling him on the phone that I needed him to come and Brian was dead.

Dad was a sales professional and very dedicated to his company. At first, he told me he couldn't come right then as he had company salesmen in town for meetings.

I couldn't believe what he was saying!

I needed him to be there for me, more than I had ever needed him at any point in my life, *and work was more important than this?*

Looking back, maybe he was in denial, shock, or both.

It was such a shock to everyone, no one ever expected something like this to happen.

This only happened to other people, not us!

But it did, and I realized this was now my new reality and I had to figure out how to survive.

Thank God, after the initial shock wore off, Dad realized the situation and made the drive to be with me the next day.

Dad and I found a letter on Brian's desk that he had written before he took his own life.

It was a long letter telling me he loved me, that I made him happy, and that he wanted me to move on and to be happy, but he couldn't go on.

Why?

Was he sick?

Had he done something wrong and couldn't live with himself?

What could be so bad that he felt he had to leave us all?

I've read the letter several times trying to find the answer. *How did I not see something?*

How could I not have known that something was horribly wrong?

Should I have been able to intervene and prevent this at the last minute?

Believe me, I've dissected and picked apart the days, nights, weeks and months before that terrible day, and I have no answer.

The only abnormal behavior that I had seen up to that point, was that he had been having bad headaches, and some days he didn't want to get out of bed to go to work.

I remember one day I came home from work and he had been sitting on the sofa all day, he said he didn't feel up to going to work.

Was he suffering from depression?

Were the headaches the cause of the depression, or was it two separate issues?

I never came up with an answer.

I remember touching and smelling his clothes as I looked through his closet, searching for what would be his burial clothes.

I didn't want to do this…why was I doing this?

When is he going to walk through the door and tell me he's home?

I had so many unanswered questions. I felt horrible for his family, I felt horrible for my family, I felt horrible myself, and I needed answers.

How do you wake up one day and decide, *this is going to be my last day?*

How do you leave the people that love you?

We all loved him so much, *how could he think it was ok to leave us?*

The immediate family viewing was held in Mishawaka, Indiana, at the funeral home where Brian's body was prepared for burial.

My mom, dad, brother, and sister arrived to stay with me at our house where Brian had killed himself. I slept fitfully in our bed the next couple of nights.

My family and I drove to the funeral home where I would see him for the first time since the EMTs took him from the ambulance into the hospital. I remember walking into the funeral home and seeing the double doors leading into the viewing parlor closed.

When the doors were opened, I saw Brian's head lying on the pillow. My knees collapsed and I would have fallen to the floor if Dad had not caught me.

When I regained my composure, we walked slowly towards the casket. It was at that point I saw Brian's face for the first time since attempting CPR on him in the garage.

The finality of his death was right there in front of me. I remember touching his hand and it was hard and cold.

After the viewing, we all left and drove to Brian's hometown of Galesburg, Illinois, for the burial.

Mom, Dad and I all stayed in the same room at the Holiday Inn. Extended family from both sides drove to Galesburg from different states. Our families arrived and came into the hotel lobby where we were gathered, looking at me with such sadness in their eyes, and I had no answers.

From that point on, my memory of the visitation is very foggy and I remember very little of it.

I do remember sitting in the very front row of seats, straight in front of his open casket, and I felt like everyone was looking at me.

I remember the awful, conflicting feelings of guilt and a complete lack of any knowledge of why he did this to himself, me, and ultimately, his entire family.

At one point, I felt as if all our family on both sides were thinking the same thing…*she knows why he did this.*

Yet, even though it was a complete shock to me, it would take many years before those feelings would subside. They never, ever went completely away.

To this day, I have no memory of the church funeral service…none.

Before the burial I began to get very sick, as if I had a severe bout of the flu.

I was vomiting, had diarrhea, cramps, and severe pain. I was in no shape to get into a car at all, much less make the drive in the funeral procession to the cemetery.

I just couldn't muster the strength mentally or physically to leave the hotel and attend the burial.

During my sickness, I had severe bleeding and passed what appeared to be a very large blood clot.

I called Mom to the bathroom and she told me I may have just miscarried a baby.

I still feel guilt to this day that I didn't escort Brian to his final resting place at the cemetery, next to his grandfather.

As I write this, tears stream down my face, and I feel anxious and weak. Reliving this is still so hard, even after all these years. But it's necessary for me to share this to help you to understand the wall I had built around myself, and to understand the struggles I faced before ever allowing myself to fall in love again.

After all, this tragedy eventually led me to my husband Steve.

At twenty years old, I experienced something unimaginable. *I would turn twenty-one a month after his death and I was now a widow. Tough times for a kid.*

We packed up the home Brian and I had bought six months prior, and I moved to Memphis to live with my parents until I was strong enough to get out on my own.

I was desperate to understand his decision, and how he could have done this to me.

I thought he loved me.

Several days after Brian's death, my dad found a letter in Brian's briefcase as he was going through his personal belongings, attempting to help me handle the bills and Brian's personal affairs.

Dad didn't want me to read it, but later decided maybe I should.

Brian's letter was addressed to a woman he met on one of his business trips, telling her that he had fallen in love with her at first sight, and that they were soul mates, etc.

My heart broke even more as I read the letter.

How could I not have known any of this?

Now along with my pain, I felt great anger.

Who really was this man, the one I thought I knew so well and loved so much?

I needed help dealing with this, so I started attending Survivors of Suicide meetings where I would sit and listen to others tell the story of their loved one that had left them too.

A statement I heard often that struck me the most was, "Suicide is one of the most selfish acts a person can commit, that they think of no one other than themselves when they make the final decision to take their own life."

They escape their pain and leave others behind to suffer for years with feelings of guilt for not knowing the thoughts in their mind, and not being able to help or stop them.

I wore my wedding ring for almost two years, it was easier that way.

When I had to divulge that I was a widow, I lied, telling people he was killed in a car accident.

If I told them how he really died, they asked too many questions and it tore open raw wounds in my heart.

I honestly didn't have the answers. I was living a lie, but it was the only way I could figure out how to make it through each day.

I did what I had to do to begin my healing and to somehow move on with my life without him.

I was honestly just trying to survive.

On the day that I found him, I pulled into the driveway around five-thirty PM.

To this day I get an uneasy, anxious feeling around that time every damn day. I think it was such a shock to my body, that it has stayed with me all these years.

Time has healed, but I won't ever forget the images of that day for as long as I live.

I wish I could.

Even today, Steve knows I can't stand the smell of exhaust fumes. I cover my nose and it feels like my skin is crawling.

Flashbacks?

I don't know, but the noxious smell still reminds me of that day in vivid detail.

A couple of years ago, I finally told our boys about this time in my life and explained that there's a reason why I worry so much about them and want them to never be afraid talk to me.

How can you love someone, be so close, and not have any idea what's going on in their head?

I've always been afraid that if the boys were going through something difficult, I might miss it.

I've lived with the fear that they might be hurting in some way or depressed, and possibly consider doing something to hurt themselves.

It all goes back to Brian.

The thought of something happening to one of them is just unbearable. I also know what my dad meant when I was in tears one day and he said, "I wish I could fix this for you, but I can't."

When your children hurt, you desperately want to fix things and take away the pain. I don't believe there's anything harder for a parent than to see their child in pain and not be able to fix things to make them happy again.

Throughout the years I've had a dream where I see Brian across a room full of people, and I'm trying to get to him, but there's so many people to get through, that by the time I get to the other side of the room he's gone.

In the dream, I'm so happy to see him and yet so upset that I can't get to him.

When I do see Brian again someday, I'll ask him, *why?*

Maybe then I'll know and be at peace with his decision.

I do feel like a survivor.

It was a painful time in my life, but I truly believe the hardship I experienced during that time gave me the strength I'd need to be married to Steve, a Navy SEAL.

It taught me how precious life is and how grateful I am that this road led me to Steve and to be blessed with our two sons. I do believe "all things happen for a reason."

There must be a reason we sometimes go through these gut-wrenching times, betrayal, struggles, and grief. I believe God has a bigger plan, and at the time we don't know it, or even believe that such a plan could exist, but it's there.

I wasn't aware of it back then, but now with that life experience behind me, I see things differently.

Now, I can't imagine my life without Steve and our sons.

I was blessed to have Brian in my life, but he left scars on my heart and a tremendous burden I carried alone for five years before I met Steve.

I don't believe he did it to hurt me or make *me* suffer, I truly believe *HE was suffering.*

For that I've forgiven him.

Now, I feel blessed that tragedy led me to meet Steve, move on with my life, and most of all, for the gift of our two sons.

CHAPTER 3

AFFIRMATIONS

*"What seems to us as bitter trials are
often blessings in disguise."*
—OSCAR WILDE

I OFTEN HAD DOUBTFUL THOUGHTS about writing this book. However, I had an affirmation recently while having my hair done that gave me the nudge I needed.

My hair stylist Joy is a single mom struggling through her own ups and downs of being a mother, working full time, and finding love again.

She introduced me to a young Marine wife at the wash bowl who had just moved to the Virginia Beach area recently.

Joy knows Steve was in the Teams through our regular talks about life when she does my hair.

Both Joy and the young Marine wife began asking me questions about how I survived as a military wife, being alone all the time, dealing with deployments, bills, working, and raising two boys.

I had this feeling the young Marine wife was struggling to learn the military lifestyle, and so Joy began asking me questions she thought might help her.

Q "How did you survive without a cell phone, Skype, email, and no communications?"
A "Well, I didn't know any different. He would leave, and I didn't know when he would be back, where he was going, and I knew I wouldn't hear from him unless he had access to a landline phone where he could call me. I just focused on getting through each day with the boys until he called or came home."

Making sure the boys had busy days helped them stay occupied and made the days go by faster for me.

They were my focus, even when I was dead exhausted.

I had to keep going because I had no other choice, especially with no family in the local area, or even within a thousand miles that could take the boys for a day, so I could just have a moment to relax and do something for me.

Q "Did you worry about him cheating on you?"
A "Well yes…the thought entered my mind on a regular basis, but I honestly didn't have the time or strength to worry about it."

Deep in my heart I knew Steve loved the boys and I, and wouldn't risk losing us. However, I must admit at times, that demon haunted me, especially after I had learned Brian had cheated on me.

I told them, "I had to just trust he would do the right thing, I really had no control over it, and had to put it out of my mind or it would drive me crazy."

I had heard stories of cheating from other wives, but just hoped our family wouldn't be affected by it.

Q "Did you ever leave him or separate?"
A "No."

Q "Are you kidding me?"
A "No, never."

When I said my wedding vows I meant them, and I had always wanted a family...a strong family that would stick together.

Yes, there were times I wanted to pack up the boys and leave, but to go where? I never wanted to give up on our little family we had made and I didn't want that for the boys.

I had already gone through so much in my life to find love again and to have my first child finally at the age of twenty-nine, that I wasn't going to give up.

I had to live this life for our boys. They deserved a secure, loving home.

Q "Did you ever get marriage counseling?"
A "No, maybe we should have several times, but we somehow made it through the hard times and kept moving forward."

It's not something I'm against, I guess we never had the time, or maybe we just believed we would work through it together.

Q "Did you ever feel resentment towards him?"
A "Yes, of course." How can you not, when you're doing everything alone and he comes and goes, and doesn't have to worry about things at home?

He knew I would take care of whatever came my way at home. I believed I had to, so he could leave and go do his job and not have to worry about me, the boys, or the house.

Q "When he did call, did you want to break down or be mad?"
A "Oh yeah, I wanted to tell him every detail of my days and how hard they were, but I also didn't want to break down on the phone, have him worry, and possibly be distracted from what he needed to do with a clear mind."

I knew how important the work he and his team were doing, and he needed to concentrate on that and not worry about us.

Joy smiled and said, "You are a fucking Unicorn!"

A Unicorn?

Wow! That's something I've never been called before.

I guessed it would be a compliment since they don't exist. Then I got brave and decided to ask them a question, "I've thought about writing a book, and if I did, would you guys be interested in reading it?"

They both said, "Yes, absolutely!" and at that moment I knew I had to finish this book.

If it helps one wife navigate through the difficulties of being a military wife and mother, then I'm happy.

I had no marriage instruction manual, no training, no guidelines, and no experience in military culture or living in a military town.

It was a challenge to say the least, but we've made it, and after twenty-six years we're still a family, and for that I'm proud I didn't give up.

The young Marine wife told me she reads anything she can to help her stay positive and give her strength. She said she highlights, tags the page, and makes notes to refer to.

I realized that even today, military wives are searching for strength, guidance, and people like themselves who are facing the same struggles.

It's sad, but true.

Many are too afraid to reach out for help, they want to be strong and often feel like they're in it all alone when he's gone.

What many don't realize is that they're NOT alone.

I too was one of those wives. I wanted to show my husband, family, and neighbors that I could do it all, when in reality, I was desperate for someone to reach out and ask me, *how are YOU doing?*

Since moving back to Virginia Beach, I've attended social gatherings with the younger generation of Team wives, and many ask me the same questions.

They want someone to tell them how to deal with the long deployments, constant training schedules, the never-ending days of being alone and taking care of everything themselves.

I've left these events wishing I could help each one of these ladies in some way. I've given my phone number to many should they need help with anything, or just someone to talk to.

I empathize with them because I've been there, and I can directly relate to much of what they're feeling and struggling with.

I realize much has changed since my husband retired, but in many ways, so many things are still the same.

"Yes...It's going to be o.k. You are going to make it through this. Stay positive and strong...Keep looking for the bright side...And always...Keep going."
–Heather Stillufsen

CHAPTER 4

How Our Story Began

"Life is not measured by the number of breaths we take,
but by the moments that take our breath away."
—Unknown

WHEN BRIAN DIED I FELT AS THOUGH God was punishing me and I had no idea why. What I know now is that God was also preparing me for the next chapter of my life.

During the time of Brian's death and prior to meeting Steve, I had to learn to function on my own, alone.

I had never lived by myself.

So, I started out with renting my first apartment at twenty-one and joined Northwest Airlines to become a flight attendant.

Traveling was new to me, including staying in a hotel room alone. My security blanket was familiar voices on TV. The Good Morning America cast became like family to me, and I depended on those voices to help me not feel so lonely each morning.

I had to learn how to live on my own and without him.

I remember going to a "shrink" and telling him I was fine when I was in the airplane working, but when I was home alone I felt afraid and had experienced panic attacks.

He told me when I was working in the airplane I knew what I was doing, what I had to do, and I was somewhat in control of my surroundings. He said when I was at home, I couldn't control my surroundings, causing my anxiety.

That made sense to me, but it didn't cure my panic attacks.

He had me look out of his office window in a tall professional building overlooking Memphis and asked me, "Can you control anything out there?"

I said, "No" and then he said, "You have to learn that sometimes we don't have any control over what happens in life, and we have to learn to handle what happens to us and live with it the best we can."

I learned slowly that I was okay living alone. I loved my job and I made great money. I've always liked airports for some reason. I love to watch people, ponder where they are going, and who they might be going to see.

I enjoyed meeting all the passengers and talking with them if time allowed. I loved meeting the celebrities that were occasionally on flights I worked. I never asked for autographs, but it was exciting to meet movie stars, professional athletes, and rockers like Ted Nugent, who Brian loved, ironically.

I wish I had kept a journal, it's so hard to recall everyone now. Some of the stars I met include Sean Connery, Gene Kelly, Joe Walsh, and Robert Plant.

Some were much nicer and more approachable than others, and some not so much. Dolly Parton was one of the nicest and most sincere, she was just like she appears on TV. After all, they're just people like you and me, all with their own unique personalities.

I missed Brian.

The pain and loneliness lived inside of me each day as I adapted to being alone and learned to put one foot in front of the other by myself.

I remember something I read somewhere, which played on a constant loop in my head, never quite going away, *"Time is the only thing that can heal, and in time the pain will ease, but it doesn't mean you'll ever forget."*

By the time I met Steve, I had built a wall around myself.

I never wanted to go through something like that again, and if I never fell in love again, I wouldn't have to.

Well, as the old saying goes, *some things we just don't have any control over.*

One Friday night, my good friend and co-worker Felicia and I decided to go to happy hour together. It was a two-for-one special, and I was walking through the crowded bar holding my two drinks when I literally bumped into Steve trying to get through the crowd to get his two drinks.

The mutual attraction was immediate, and after apologizing we began to talk for a long while, we danced closely, and I felt something I had not felt since Brian died.

He introduced me to his group of "friends." I asked him what they were all doing there and where they worked.

I honestly don't remember what he told me, but it was not "we're Navy SEALS." We all hung out talking and laughing, then later that night, Steve excused himself to the restroom.

One of his buddies, a very handsome and fit Hawaiian-looking guy named Tony informed me that Steve was gay, and I should just plan on going out on a date with him instead.

I thought, *well, okay then, nothing wrong with that, but it seems to be just my luck.*

Through my job as a flight attendant, I had worked with several good-looking gay men who were also flight attendants. One of my closest friends was a handsome gay man. Not unusual, right?

So, when he returned, I hid my disappointment, and just came right out and asked him if he was gay. All his buddies burst out laughing as he fired off a string of profanities at Tony with his buddies laughing even harder.

I was relieved.

When the night came to an end, he walked Felicia and I out to the car and then proceeded to climb into the back seat like he knew where he was going, very much unable to drive anywhere.

I asked him what he was doing, and he said, "I'm going home with you!" and I said, "No you're not!"

I wasn't ready for that just yet in my healing process.

He had no idea what I had been through, and I had no idea who he really was, *or why he was in Memphis.*

And most importantly of all, I was not that type of girl. After all, we had only just met several hours earlier.

Little did I know how different my life would look only one year later. I did know something very special had happened that night as I looked into his deep blue eyes for the first time, and somehow, I also knew I would marry that man.

It was a difficult relationship for a while. I was flying, and he was traveling all over the country training with his team.

I now knew he was a Navy SEAL, but was still unsure what that meant exactly. I knew he jumped out of airplanes, shot all kinds of guns, used explosives, worked out and swam a lot, and other than that, I really didn't know much about his job.

We carried on a long-distance relationship for several months as I lived in Memphis and him in Virginia Beach. We saw each other when we could, and I would come to Virginia Beach more often because I had my employee passes to fly for free into Norfolk.

He would take me to "Team Parties" as his girl. Most of these parties were uncomfortable for me to say the least. The guys were always nice to me, but several of the long-time wives and girlfriends not so much, most of the time.

I could feel the eyes looking at me, as if to say,

Who is she?

Where did she come from?

How long will she last?

There were women out there that specifically wanted to date or marry a SEAL, and not even knowing what a Navy SEAL really was, I certainly wasn't one of them.

Some girls were completely okay with being a groupie, they loved the party scene, the hard bodies, and the lifestyle.

That wasn't me. It doesn't make me better than anyone else, it's just not who I was or ever wanted to be.

I loved Steve for who he was as a man, not because he was a SEAL. I would tell myself not to let it bother me, as they had no idea who I was or what I had been through.

Like most everyone, I've always wanted people to like me and have always tried to treat people how I want to be treated, but some of these parties were a challenge for me.

For a new woman coming into the team, it seemed to be a much more welcoming climate around the guys than the women, at least for the first year or so.

Once we were married, many wives accepted me into the community and made me feel welcome, and eventually I learned to understand where they were coming from.

They were protective of their husbands, boyfriends, and their tight-knit community.

After our first year of a serious relationship I felt I could trust Steve, I loved him and knew he loved me. Next thing I know, I've packed my belongings into a U-Haul truck and moved to Virginia.

So, what got me to move to Virginia?

Well, back in Memphis one night in my apartment, as I was picking out an outfit to wear to dinner, Steve came into my walk-in closet, kissed me tightly, and proposed!

Yes, in my closet.

Not the most romantic proposal, but in his own way, I guess he couldn't wait, and I was beyond happy to say yes!

It was just Steve being himself, and I loved him for it.

When I arrived in Virginia Beach, I had not previously seen the condo that he had picked for us to live in, so I really didn't know what I was coming into, but it was a nice little place.

It was very small and nearly empty as if unoccupied, but it was clean and had a small patio and a little pond along the back yard.

I had moved an apartment full of furniture, dishes, and accessories, and was a bit surprised when I walked in for the first time.

For his furnishings, Steve had basic cookware and kitchen tools, a few ammo crates stacked into tables and night stands, several metal footlockers full of different uniforms and equipment, a futon bed, his beloved Navy web gear and rucksack, and that was about it.

With some work and creativity, I quickly made our little condo into our home.

We both came and went according to our work schedules, meeting up at the condo as much as possible. When we were both home, we would cook dinner together and drink wine in our tiny kitchen.

When I had layovers in Seattle, I would bring home fresh crab legs or salmon from Pike Place Market on dry ice to surprise him. We enjoyed just spending time together and we didn't have to go out. Our time was so limited together that we just wanted to be alone in our little home.

During this time, I got a taste of what my life was going to look like as a SEAL wife.

I spent many nights alone in that condo.

For some reason, I would ease the loneliness by telling myself it would get better and he would be home more.

I really thought it would be temporary and that once we were married things would change.

Boy, was I wrong.

But, it had been several years since I had felt so loved, in love and happy, so I wasn't going to let his absence ruin our relationship.

Flying kept my mind occupied and me busy. I remember talking to him on pay phones in airports in between flights, at the first chance of possibly connecting on a landline.

When he was away training and staying in a hotel, I could call him and just hearing his voice was such a comfort.

At the time, Steve's unit was training and rehearsing for Desert Storm and he was away a lot more than usual.

I had no idea of the types of missions his unit was training for, which was probably a good thing for my own sanity.

I was greeting passengers on a flight one afternoon in January of 1991 after we had just married only a few weeks earlier, when a passenger walked on and said to me, "We're going to war."

I said, "What?" and he repeated himself again, "Yes, we're going to war," as I stood there unable to move.

I knew Steve would have to deploy. When the beeper went off or they got a special briefing at work, they were usually on planes, flying out of Virginia only a few hours later.

I thought *I have to get off this airplane and call him.*

Will I see him before he leaves?

This can't be happening, we just got married...*when will I see him again?*

I couldn't get off the airplane to call him and I worked the flight in a numb state, with my mind everywhere except on my job.

Thank God, the war was over quickly, and his unit didn't have to do the high risk, extremely dangerous missions they had trained for. He came home safe to me, and for that, I'm grateful.

When we lived at the condo I had to compete for his time with his hobby, or should I call it his escape activity?

I would call him from my trips and he would be over at his buddy's house until all hours of the night, working on his 1970 Dodge Demon race car he had built.

We had several arguments about this. I felt a sense of jealousy about this car, he spent much of his off time working on it. Remember, there were no cell phones back then and when I called, the landline would ring and ring, with no answer.

I had no idea that I would be competing for his time with a project, and this would continue for many more years to come.

I've heard this from other Team wives too, and it seems like all these guys have something they tinker with.

Is it to forget what they're doing at work?

Is it to just let their mind relax and focus on something other than work?

Is it an escape activity?

Or is it how they relieve stress and clear their head, so they can be fully ready for the next task?

I didn't know the answer then, and I don't think I do now.

I knew I loved him, he loved me, and hopefully things would get better if we gave it more time.

Our story was only just beginning.

CHAPTER 5

I Do

"Let go and let God…."

—UNKNOWN ORIGIN

STEVE AND I WERE MARRIED on December 29, 1990, during an ice storm in Des Moines, Iowa. We had a small beautiful wedding in the Des Moines Botanical Garden. Our closest friends and family came in from all over the United States to share our special day. Many were meeting Steve for the first time, but I was confident that they would love him just as much as I did. It was an emotional, happy day.

As Steve was saying his vows, he began his "nervous laugh" that he could hardly contain and I thought, *Oh my God, he is not going to make it through this without bursting into his loud, hardy laugh.*

It took every bit of self-control he had to not burst into laughter. Such a serious moment during a wedding ceremony…and my husband could hardly contain himself.

That was hardly the way Dad described Steve when he warned me about marrying him.

I will never forget when Dad learned we were going to be married and asked me, "Do you know he is professionally trained to lie and kill?"

I never thought of it that way. I think Dad was concerned about Steve being like a trained spy in the military and of course the dangers of being a SEAL.

I knew he worried for me and never wanted to see me go through the pain again I had endured when Brian died.

Over the years Dad and Steve have formed a very close bond, and Steve thinks of Dad as his dad, and I know Dad loves him as a son.

We both had to get back to our jobs right away after the wedding and so our honey moon followed several months later.

I was learning quickly we would be living around his work schedule, and to be together, I would need to plan my trips according to his schedule.

Thank goodness, I had that flexibility in my job. At the time, I also made more money than he did. At first this was kind of awkward, but it helped us to buy our first home, a boat, travel, and do things we may not have been able to without my income.

He was an E-5 when we got married, and E-5 pay wasn't a lot of money, even with his jump, dive, and specialty pays. It would have been tough to live on his salary alone, and we were now what some might call "DINKs"—Dual Income, No Kids.

We had a lot of fun flying around on my passes, $20 co-pay for First Class, $10 co-pay for Coach. Steve thought he was a high-roller, sitting up in the First Class cabin in his sport coat and tie, drinking Mai-Tais and being waited on by the Flight Attendants.

About two years after we were married, our first son Nate was born, and little did we know, our carefree traveling lifestyle was about to change.

In early 1992, I was commuting to Detroit to attend our yearly FAA mandated training class. As I sat looking out the window, I had this feeling I was pregnant.

I told myself I would buy a pregnancy test when I got back home. Steve was home when I got back, and I went into the bathroom to take the test and sure enough it was positive.

I sat down on the side of the tub and just starred at the test thinking, *Oh my God, I'm pregnant.*

I was happy and nervous at the same time. I opened the door and looked at Steve and said, "We're going to have a baby." He laughed his nervous laugh and was just as excited and surprised as I was.

I flew until I was six months along wearing the airline uniform maternity dress with the attractive expandable waistline. During my sixth month, it was beginning to really drain me.

Pulling those heavy beverage carts up the aisle and long hours on my feet was taking its toll. To top it off, I had to commute from Norfolk to Detroit just to get to work to start my trip, and then fly back to Norfolk again to return home. It became exhausting.

I was hoping I could find someone to take care of our baby, so I could continue flying after it was born.

I envisioned using my passes and taking the baby to meet all our family when it was old enough, and I could picture the family trips we would make in the future years.

We had no family around and so my search began. I was going to have to find someone to love and take care of him or her for several days at a time while we were both gone.

I was twenty-nine, and at one point thought I may never be married again and have children, so whomever would take care of my baby had to be extra special.

I never found that person.

I would leave almost every interview with a sick feeling in my stomach, knowing it didn't feel right and I needed to trust my gut instinct.

I couldn't count on Steve. He was on call 24/7 every day of the year and could be called away anytime of the day or night without warning.

I had to go into this search as if I were a single parent.

When he was at home, he was always on different alert cycles for twelve weeks at a time. Every third cycle, he was on a one-hour recall status.

He also carried the faithful command beeper on his belt 24/7. When the damned thing went off, we'd have to stop whatever we were doing, he would grab his "ready bag" of spare clothes and whatever else he always carried, and there he went. Heading into base, there was no text messages or last-minute phone conversations during the drive...beepers were a one-way communication device.

Also, once he arrived inside the compound, there were no more phone calls out if they were heading out on a mission.

If I got lucky, he would return home several hours later because it was a drill, or they didn't get a deployment order from the big brass in Washington.

When he left on these recalls, I rarely knew where he was going and whether I would see him in three days, three weeks, or three months.

On one occasion he was on leave hunting Caribou on the Northern Slope of Alaska. Somehow, he was recalled when his group had stopped for fuel and supplies at a wilderness truck stop in Coldfoot.

He had no idea how his command could find him on leave, hunting up in the Arctic Circle, timing their call so that it caught him when he was actually stopped at the only landline phone 250 miles each way from Fairbanks and Prudhoe Bay.

It had to have been pure luck.

How the hell did the government pull that off?

His hunting buddy, Uncle Tom, who was always like a dad to Steve, drove him 250 miles to the Fairbanks airport, seven hours south. He got on the next flight out of Fairbanks, switched planes several times on the way, and landed later at Norfolk International with his ruck, gear, and rifle.

I picked him up at the airport and we went directly home where he ate dinner with baby Nate and me, grabbed his ready bag, gun, and gear, and drove off to catch another flight out to an aircraft carrier off the coast of Virginia.

He returned home over ninety days later.

Several times he would leave after being recalled, and I had no idea where he was going, or when he would be home.

Once again, I was alone.

Who has this kind of job, with a commitment that comes before family and everything else in life?

Who could fill a position like that?

During the interview process of finding a nanny, I worried about all the things that could go wrong if the baby got sick and I was across the country on a trip. How long would it take me to get home? I had to take all the scenarios seriously, it was our life.

I made the decision to resign.

I had waited too long to be a mom.

My career would need to come to an end to allow Steve to have his career and come and go as he needed to.

Did I regret that decision? At times I did, I missed the income, the job itself, and the travel passes, but I loved every minute of raising my boys. If I had it to do over again, I would choose to be with them and not miss out on the many joys and special times we would have together over the years.

I felt they needed security in their little lives. It was hard enough with Steve gone as much as he was. They needed stability and routine.

At the very least, they needed their mother to be there for them 24/7.

It was going to be a financial strain to take a huge pay cut after we had just purchased a home and established our dual income lifestyle.

But the interviews convinced me beyond a shadow of a doubt that the mother my kids would need full time at home, was me.

I don't think we realized the impact of the pay cut until months later when we were broke, with a big stack of bills sitting on the kitchen counter.

I would need to leave a job I loved and felt so lucky to have. That job helped me heal and to move on with my life. It was because that job required me to be based out of Memphis, that I met Steve.

I felt I had no other option…Steve could not give up his job for my career. He had just joined a new unit and volunteered to serve there for at least another six years.

No, I made the right choice—staying at home to raise the children I had waited for all my life.

———∿———

"Childhood is a short season."
–HELEN HAYES

———∿———

CHAPTER 6

Spouse Indoc

"Breathe darling. This is just a chapter.
Its not your whole story."
–S.C. Lourie

S OMETIME IN 1991, not long after Steve and I were married, he
came home one day and told me that I had to go to a mandatory
meeting soon at the command for all wives.

If I were still his fiancé or girlfriend, I wouldn't have been allowed
to attend. No, this was only for wives — Steve told me it was "Spouse
Indoc," short for Spouse Indoctrination.

Not having a military background, I had no idea what it was all
about, and Steve was very secretive about things he discussed and
casual conversations in general. I thought it would be like a social
gathering, not a party, but maybe a get-together for the new wives to
meet up and get to know one another.

Not so much.

This would be the beginning of my indoctrination to the new
life for a SEAL wife.

The meeting was hosted by his Commanding Officer, the Captain. He told us, "You're not to discuss your husband's job on the phone, and don't tell people like friends and neighbors where your husband works, because this compound doesn't exist to the public."

What?

"You can say he is in the Navy, but don't mention SEAL, his work location, and never expect your husband to tell you where he's going or when he'll be back."

I remember leaving the building and thinking…*okay then, this is going to be very interesting. What in the hell have I gotten myself into?*

Yeah, as a military newcomer, I was pretty much scared into not saying anything about what he really did or where he worked, for fear I would get him in trouble. Steve had told me all his Commanding Officers and many of the more senior Master Chiefs were SEALs or Underwater Demolition Team members in Vietnam.

He said, "Those are guys to be respected, real badasses that spent whole year-long deployments living and fighting the Viet Cong in the jungle."

At that time, outside of their community, it was completely different than it is now…SEALs were relatively unknown.

As a flight attendant when fellow crew members would ask what my husband did, I would feel a lump in my throat and tell them, "He's in the Navy."

"What does he do?" At first, I struggled with the right answer and would say something like, "Um, he's a support guy."

"Where is he based?"

"Oh, at Little Creek," and most of the time, lucky for me, that would answer their questions enough to satisfy their curiosity.

I did tell a select few the truth if I felt I could trust them, like our pilots who had been in the Navy themselves.

Often, they read between the lines before I told them and would say, "Oh, he's a SEAL?" and I would nod my head.

I would then feel a rush of guilt come over me, as if I had committed a terrible sin and the Captain was going to find out and I would have to answer to him for not following directions. Then my husband would be punished for what I had just said.

I felt like I lived a secretive existence.

I didn't want to do anything wrong or say anything that I wasn't supposed to.

That Captain had put the fear of God in me.

After all, I married into a life that I honestly knew nothing about. I didn't grow up in a military family, and had only heard about the Navy SEALs on a National Geographic show. I remember thinking, *wow, that's a crazy job.*

After Steve was no longer a new guy and had established himself within the command, we had both grown to respect and love his Commanders. They were like military father figures to he and I both, especially after I got more involved with the command and other families socially. We had great times volunteering to help with command functions and the annual Christmas party.

Then Steve created an annual monster of our own. He decided to invite all his sniper team buddies to a private Christmas party at our house. This got out of control every year when several wouldn't leave. Together with Steve, they had decided that their little party with the remaining three or four guys was not ending until ALL the beer was gone and ALL the liquor bottles were empty. The music would get louder and louder, waking the babies and I, and they were not nice to me if I came downstairs and asked them to quiet down.

Usually I woke to a mess in the kitchen and several drunken SEAL snipers, all in Christmas sweaters, including Steve, passed out all over the kitchen or living room floor. Steve would apologize to me if he had hurt my feelings by saying something rude when he was trashed, then he would start to clean up. Luckily, he and most of the other guys matured, growing out of the hard-core binge drinking as they got older.

Every time he returned home, I would finally get a phone call that he was back from wherever and to come pick him up at work. I would load up the boys in their car seats, sometimes getting them out of bed, as it could be any time of the day or night.

His military flights usually came in at one of the local airports and a bus would transport the guys and their bags back to the compound.

The boys and I would wait patiently in my vehicle in the parking lot outside of a chain-link fence with a gate guard. Eventually he would come walking out with his backpack on his back and a big smile on his face.

The homecomings were always a little like a first date. I would even get nervous, because I had so many emotions.

Do I look ok?

Have I gained weight?

Is he as happy to see me as I am him?

Will I cry?

I have so much to tell him, where do I start?

How much time will I have with him until he has to leave again?

I wanted to know what he had been doing and where he had been. I knew he couldn't tell me, so I didn't ask. I was just happy he made it back to us safely and we could be a family for a few days or weeks until it was time to drop him off again.

Not much time would pass, and I would drop him off at the command. Once more, I would drive the same route home with tears streaming down my face, preparing myself yet again to be alone with the boys, not knowing when he would return.

The boys were young when he was at that command, and I would tell them every day that Daddy had to go to work, he would be back as soon as he could, and that he loved them. I would then mentally prepare myself to face whatever challenges would come during this time away.

As we military wives know…If something is going to break down, leak, or malfunction in some way, it will happen when he is gone.

That's just how it is.

Such things may include broken bones, stitches, illness, air conditioner or heat going out, water heater rupturing, etc.

If it can go wrong, it usually will when Daddy is away.

Steve was away on a trip when little Luke had to have a plastic surgeon reattach the end of his finger. He and his brother were arguing when Nate slammed the door on Luke's finger that was in the door hinge. We lived outside of Brunswick, Maine, at the time. Once again, we had no family to call for help, only my good friend and neighbor, Annette, who lived across the street.

I frantically called her on the landline, and she came running over as I attempted to stop the bleeding and get him into the car.

I remember being extremely angry, thinking, *here we are on shore duty and Steve is not even in the state.*

He and his fellow SEAL Mike had just left for Virginia the day before to give some pre-deployment briefings to a fighter squadron.

The Brunswick hospital flew in a pediatric plastic surgeon from Portland to perform the surgery, as the tip of his middle finger was only hanging by a bit of skin. The doctor did a wonderful job and Luke recovered quickly, even though it was painful for a three-year old.

However, I was emotionally drained and traumatized by the shock of seeing my baby boy in such pain and being rushed into surgery. I was angry at Nate for doing this to his brother, and angry at Steve for not being there for us during this crisis.

Later I had to calmly talk to Nate and explain to him what had happened to Luke and what he had gone through, all because Nate didn't want Luke in his room. Even after this traumatic injury, the brotherly spats would continue for many years to come.

I should've learned to ask for help. I wasn't Wonder Woman and I wish I would've asked. I now know there were many nice people willing back then as there are now, I just didn't want to, know how, or really, who to ask.

The boys would both get sick at the same time, the washer would break down, the lawnmower would quit, the garbage disposal would stop working, you name it…it's just what happens.

Thank goodness things are now much different. There are far more resources and social channels available to reach out to for a hand or someone to talk to during deployments.

I experienced my first Virginia hurricane when Steve was gone as well. I listened to the news and stocked up on food, water, batteries, and filled my gas tank.

I remember thinking, *oh my God this is going to be terrible.*

I was scared to death. I had no idea what to expect. My neighbor came over and helped me secure our patio furniture. He told me to stay away from the windows during the storm and to sleep downstairs, so we would be better protected if a tree fell on the house.

I remember thinking, *great! How in the hell does he manage to always be gone during this crap?*

I set up Nate's playpen in the living room, brought his mattress downstairs from his crib, made a bed for myself on the sofa, and covered his playpen with the mattress. It was more of a comfort for me than a safe way to protect him as he slept, but it was the only thing I could think of at the time.

Now that I think of it, that was probably a dumb thing to do, but I wanted to protect him should the windows shatter or a tree fell on the house.

I didn't know how to prepare for a hurricane, and once again, there I was, being a good military wife and just doing the best I could.

"What doesn't kill you makes you stronger."
–FRIEDRICH NIETZSCHE

CHAPTER 7

BLESSED

"The day you came into my life, I knew what my purpose
was. To love and protect with everything I have."
—LIVING AND LOVING SA

O UR FIRST SON WAS BROUGHT INTO THE WORLD
October 31st, 1992. I called him our Halloween Treat!

Nate was a beautiful, healthy baby, and I had never felt such immediate love. I remember when Doctor Holly held up our baby and said, "It's a boy!" The first thing I saw was his big hands and remember her laughing because he had peed all over her scrubs.

Steve was beyond happy to learn we had a boy and so was I. I was scared, excited, in love, and yet nervous on becoming a new mom. I was so thankful Steve was in town and able to be at the birth of our son.

He held Nate so delicately with his big hands, he was in love with this little guy too, I could see it in his eyes. I had just come out of recovery, they were monitoring my heart and blood pressure when my happiness turned to fear.

Yes, the damn beeper went off, and he had to leave Nate and I at the hospital and go into work. He hugged me and told me this was a real recall and he may not be back for a while and left the room.

Oh my God, how are we going to get home?

I just had an emergency C-section only a few hours earlier and I wasn't supposed to drive for six weeks. The doctor told me I wasn't supposed to go up or down steps, and all of Nate's things were on the second floor, as we lived in a two-story house.

We're going to have to go home alone!

That was not how I envisioned bringing our son into the world. I remember lying in the hospital bed with a full-blown anxiety attack.

I couldn't stop crying and I asked the nurse to keep Nate for a few minutes, so I could get myself together.

Once again, I had no family members there with me, and all I wanted was for one of them to walk in the room and tell me they would take us home and help me while I healed.

I NEEDED someone to tell me it would all be ok.

In my mind, I thought, *God has just given me Nate, and now he is going to take Steve away from us?*

Why?

I remember feeling deep in my soul that Steve wasn't going to come home alive, and I would be left to raise Nate alone without his dad.

I felt this in my gut. I hurt so deeply inside, I just knew I wasn't going to see him again, that something terrible was going to happen. I had never felt this before when Steve left, never...but I did this time, and I believed my gut feeling to be true.

The nurse brought Nate to me, and I held our beautiful baby close and cried, telling him his Daddy loved him, and that I would always take care of him and love him.

Several hours passed and in walked Steve with a big smile on his face. The mission had been called off at the last minute, and he couldn't tell me why or where they were supposed to be going.

I felt like I could breathe again, like I just woke up from a terrible nightmare.

Thank you God, for giving him back to us, I said under my breath.

Years later he told me the mission plan had them going into a very hostile area of Africa, possibly confirming my gut feeling was right. Between October 3-4, 1993, almost a year later after Nate was born, we lost eighteen American special operators in the Battle of Mogadishu and seventy-three were wounded in the two days of fighting.

We spent several days in the hospital and then the three of us got into our Jeep Cherokee and went home TOGETHER!

I get emotional as I'm writing this now, as it was such a roller coaster of feelings and emotions in such a short period of time.

I feared since Brian had died, I was finally happy, had a beautiful baby and a wonderful husband, that for some reason Steve was going to be taken away after he gave me Nate.

I never had that feeling again for the rest of his career, and it was the one and only time when he left that I truly felt I would never see him again.

I've believed in God my whole life and I am a Christian. I pray and talk to God daily, I believe in the power of prayer and that He answered my prayer that day.

For some unknown reason, the deployment for his team's mission was put on hold.

We pulled into the driveway of our first home with our newborn child. There was a blue wooden stork in the yard announcing Nate's arrival. I had eighteen staples, yes staples, running along my lower stomach and had to move very slowly. Thank God Steve was there to help me.

We got settled into the house, and Steve brought everything down from the nursery upstairs. Before Nate was born, I had all the baby accessories set up for his or her arrival, but now since I couldn't go up and down the steps, he had to set up a new nursery downstairs.

I breast fed Nate and would sit in the chair and look at him and cry, he was so perfect and so beautiful, he was ours, and I couldn't have been happier.

As I watched him sleep in my arms, I tried to imagine him at two or five, or as a teenager, and I just couldn't picture him anything other than what he was at that moment.

Steve went back to work, but came home every night for a while, and that was a relief. Just knowing he would be with us at the end of the day gave me peace.

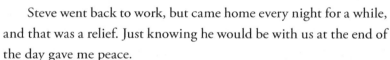

Unfortunately, that didn't last long.

He had to go out of the country for three months, but I knew he would be back this time. Of course, only days after he left I got an infection around one of the staples and had to go see Doctor Holly.

I told her I was alone and couldn't come in every day to have the infected hole in my stomach unpacked and repacked. I wasn't even supposed to be driving yet.

She arranged for a nurse to come to our home every day and take care of my wound. It was so painful, but I knew it had to be done, and all I cared about was taking care of Nate's every need.

With Steve being gone, I ended up going up and down the steps very slowly because I had no option, I just had to do it.

I finally healed up after several weeks and was beginning to feel more normal again…breast feeding and fighting the infection had taken a toll on me.

I was exhausted.

During this time, I was also mourning the loss of my dear Grandma May, who had passed away when I was in my eighth month of pregnancy.

Dr. Holly wouldn't allow me to fly to Minnesota for her funeral, she said it was too dangerous. I felt a terrible sense of loss, I missed her so much, and I missed talking with her.

She was so excited about our baby and now she would never get to meet Nate. Since I didn't get to go to her funeral, I couldn't get it through my head she was gone. I just couldn't believe that I would never see her again or hear her voice.

Nate was going to be her first great-grandchild, as I had been her first grandchild. She was having a lady in her small town make a quilt for Nate. My Aunt later sent it to me and I still have it to this day.

Steve finally came home and couldn't believe how Nate had grown and changed since he left. He would see these changes many, many times in the following years, and I knew that I had made the right decision to leave my career and stay at home to take care of our son.

I loved watching Steve interact with Nate.

He would change his diaper, clean him well, dry him off, and use lots of baby powder. He always said, "Boys don't like to have sticky balls, so we gotta make sure they're dry till he wets himself again."

When it was time to put Nate to sleep, Steve would lay out Nate's baby blanket in a diamond shape, carefully laying him in the middle and rolling him in the blanket like a cigar. He would then let Nate fall fast asleep on his chest, rolled up in his blanket.

Grandpa Tony, who was Grandma May's husband, died two years later when I was pregnant with our second child. I was very close to him as well and traveled to Minnesota for his funeral, as I was only a couple months along.

I sat in the pew during the service holding Nate, thinking how sad each had died during my pregnancies.

Every home we've lived in, I've always had a male and female Cardinal visit my bird feeders and nest somewhere in our yard. I believe it's them watching over us. Steve names them Tony and May, and it always makes me smile.

With Nate, we wanted his sex to be a surprise, even though *I just knew* I was carrying a boy. With our second baby we wanted to know ahead of time, so we could prepare the nursery, should it be a girl.

I went to my ultrasound appointment and learned we were going to have another boy. I couldn't wait to call Steve at work and tell him a second boy was on the way.

He was so happy, laughing his nervous laugh with excitement.

He called them his "Little Tadpoles."

I remember taking Nate to the beach while pregnant with Luke. I'd watch all the families having fun together and the dads playing with their little ones in the sand. I would put my hand on my belly and wish Steve could be there with us too.

He had missed most of Nate's first two years of life. Now we were bringing another baby into the world, and unfortunately, his duties would keep him from much of Luke's first years as well.

I envied those families on the beach, they looked so happy, and yet I didn't even know where my husband was or when he would be back.

Why us?

Then I'd remind myself that I had a job to do here, that Steve was doing his job, and I had to keep going and get these jealous feelings and thoughts out of my mind.

He wasn't gone because he wanted to be gone, he was gone because he was doing his job and doing what had to be done for the good of our country.

I knew he would rather be here with us on the beach if he could, and that I had to stay positive, or at least try hard to.

On February 1st, 1995, our beautiful Luke was born. Another healthy baby boy with a full head of black hair. Steve was at the birth of Luke too, and for that I was grateful.

He sat in the chair in my room and held Luke with Nate on his lap, while Nate looked at his newborn baby brother. I imagine he was wondering who he was and why his dad was holding him.

I remember worrying when I was pregnant with Luke if I could love another baby as much as I loved Nate, and *how would I share that love between the two?*

I should've never wasted time worrying about that, because my love for Luke was instant and equal the minute he was born.

I had my hands full with an infant and a two year old, and couldn't have felt happier or more blessed until my mother-in-law called and wanted to come visit to meet Luke.

She told me that she had walking pneumonia, but that she would bring a mask and wear it around Luke. I asked her not to come until she was completely over it.

Since February was the middle of flu season, I had kept Luke at home away from people, as I didn't want him to catch anything. She resisted and came anyway.

She did wear the mask, but the Doctor later told me the virus can still spread through those masks.

At four weeks old, we almost lost our beautiful Luke. We had to take him to the Children's Hospital in Norfolk and he was admitted into ICU. He had contracted Respiratory Syncytial Virus (RSV) and Pneumonia.

He was so small and so very sick. Luke was such a good baby and it killed me to watch him lie helpless in the hospital bed with wires and tubes attached all over his tiny body.

Thank God Steve was at home with Nate. Our neighbors and friends would watch Nate so Steve could come visit once in a while and bring me clean clothes. He had to wear a sterile yellow gown and mask when he came into the room to see us.

When he saw little Luke lying in a maze of wires and plastic tubes, he went out to his truck and returned with a roll of rigger's tape (green duct tape).

He routed and organized all the tubes and wires neatly, taping them together in bundles so I could pick Luke up more easily to breast feed him.

Luke didn't have an appetite, but I was determined to continue breast feeding him. I believed it would help him get stronger and recover faster.

I prayed several times a day for God to heal my precious little boy and told Him that I would do anything if he would heal Luke. I begged him in my prayers to take me, but not my baby.

Luke was in ICU for five nights. About mid-week I had fallen asleep in the chair and awoke with a feeling that someone was in the room with us.

I opened my eyes and saw a large black woman in a white dress standing over Luke with her hand on his head. I'd never seen her before and I said, "Hi," very quietly.

She looked at me, smiled, and said, "The Good Lord ain't going to take this precious baby," as she looked back down at him and continued to rub his head with her hand, smiling at him.

I remember saying, "He's going to be ok?" and she just smiled and nodded.

I never saw her again.

Luke was released on the sixth day and to this day I can still see her standing by his bed and hear her exact words in my mind.

I never knew who she was, what she did in the hospital, or why she came into his room that night.

I remember feeling a powerful sense of calm and peace when she told me Luke was going to be okay.

I told Steve about her visit and that I felt like she was an angel sent from God.

He said he felt in his heart that she probably was.

He walked all through the ICU looking for a nurse that matched her description and couldn't find her anywhere. I never saw her again either.

We could've lost Luke during that serious illness, but the little guy pulled through, and I once again thank God for that.

Nate and Luke had a brotherly love/hate relationship when they were little. They either played well together or would make each other upset and fight over the smallest things.

I think that's only normal for siblings, and for us moms it can be exhausting. I believe it's a part of growing up together, discovering themselves, and developing their own personalities.

There were times when they were young, I thought, *I just can't do this.*

But looking back, I wish I would've relaxed more, worried less, and not stressed about the small stuff.

I wish I would have "picked my battles" as they say. I wish I could replay each day of their childhood in my mind, it all went by so fast.

I remember people telling me, "Enjoy them while their young, because they grow up too fast," and I thought, *what the hell are they talking about? I feel like I'm losing my mind.*

Well, like almost all parents, I found that statement to be true. Looking back, I don't know where the years went. What I do know is; that I love my boys, I have much to be thankful for, and I'm proud to be their mom.

I loved when they lived at home and I was busy running them around to sports or activities, packing their lunch, even washing their clothes, and most importantly spending time with them.

I really miss our family dinners where I would ask them about their day and have quality time with them.

I always felt dinner was so important, to eat together as a family and talk to one another. A lot of families don't do that anymore.

I found that's when I got the most information out of them about their day, or what they were thinking about at that time. I used to ask them, "What was the best thing that happened to you today?"

They would both tell me, and then I would ask, "What was the worst thing that happened to you today?" and they would tell me that too.

I wasn't a perfect mom and I lacked in discipline at times because I felt sorry for them that their dad was gone so much. But I know I did the very best I could.

I made sure they knew I loved them and was there to protect and take care of them.

It was hard being a dad and a mom when Steve was away, but I tried to give them a good home life and a happy one.

They were my focus, and each day was devoted to what they needed, and I don't regret it one bit.

I've carried the quote below in my wallet, written on an old piece of paper for over twenty years.

———————～———————

"Each day of our lives, we make deposits in
the memory banks of our children."
—CHARLES R. SWINDOLL

———————～———————

ALL BECAUSE TWO
PEOPLE FELL IN LOVE

I Do...December 29, 1990

Cross-country skiing in my home state of Minnesota.

Steve in the Bitterroot Wilderness, early 1990's.

Steve training for a deployment.

Steve climbing sea cliffs off the coast of northern Maine.

One of my favorite photos of Steve and the boys.

The boys and I taking in nature during our road trip to Montana.

Nate and Luke on one of our day excursions in Maine.

*Virginia family photo following our shore duty in Maine,
back home for another SEAL Team tour.*

Steve and Moose on one of our few getaways in Maine.

The sheer expression of joy—a boy with his dog and the day's catch.

Even brothers get along when the fish are biting.

My happy place—spending time together out on the water.

CHAPTER 8

FRIENDS ARE CHOSEN FAMILY

"Good friends are like stars, you don't always see them, but you know they're always there."

–Designs by Kathy

BOY, IF THAT ISN'T THE TRUTH. When you don't live in the city or state that your family does, you meet people that become your friends, and many become your family.

I can honestly say I've never had a lot of girlfriends, but the ones I do have, I've had for many years and I take time to nourish these friendships because they mean so much to me.

I would rather have a few friends I completely trust, that are there through the thick and the thin, than several meaningless friendships.

I really don't know what I would have done without these relationships throughout my life.

When I started dating Steve, he wanted me to meet his married friends Jay and Laura. Jay was a parachute rigger at SEAL Team 2. They became close friends through work, and Steve didn't care he wasn't a SEAL. He said, "Jay's job is just as important, and after all, you probably want to be buddies with the guy that packs your reserve parachute."

It made me feel good Steve appreciated the support techs and their role in the Teams. It also showed me he didn't categorize people into what they did for a living, and that he didn't let his SEAL ego dictate how he treated others.

Steve had a motorcycle at the time and we rode out to a boat ramp to meet Jay and Laura for a day on the water. I was nervous to meet them and hoped I would make a good impression on his friends.

Jay smiled and was friendly. Laura looked at me and was cordial, but not overly excited to meet me.

Much later she told me she thought I was, "Just another girlfriend." We made small talk on the boat ride and I remember leaving thinking, *well, I don't think she really cares for me.*

We've now been friends for over 25 years. They became our closest friends and we had many great times together. Our friendship grew, we spent many holidays, birthdays, and happy hours together.

Laura even gave me a baby shower when I was pregnant with Nate. The four of us just hit it off, and we always looked forward to a get-together… it was an easy friendship.

When Nate was born, we knew that we wanted Jay and Laura to be his Godparents, and to be there at the Little Creek chapel with us for his baptism.

Steve and I asked them if they would do this, and it was emotional for all of us. I trusted if anything happened to Steve and me, that Jay and Laura would take him in, love him, and raise him as their own child.

I felt much comfort in knowing we had them in our lives and I knew they would always be a part of Nate's life in their responsibility as his Godparents.

We were right.

I enjoyed sharing Nate's first years of life with Laura. Jay and Laura took care of him and loved him like their own, and it made me happy that Nate had them in his life as our family was so far away.

Two years later when Luke was born, once again we asked Jay and Laura to be his Godparents also.

If something were to happen to us, we knew they would make sure the boys stayed together, no matter what.

We had this written into our Will as well for legal purposes, and to ensure they couldn't fall under state control.

We have so many happy memories with Jay and Laura. During the holidays, Laura would have the boys and I over before Christmas to bake and decorate cookies. She would wear her apron and have all the sprinkles and icings out on the counter for the boys to decorate their cookies.

It was like going to Grandma's house, and we all looked forward to it and enjoyed it. It became a tradition and I know the boys still remember those times to this day.

They also took care of the boys so Steve and I could get away or have a date night, which we needed and was much appreciated.

Since Nate was born on Halloween, we'd all get together and carve pumpkins, sometimes they would show up in full costume, which the boys loved.

They were always a part of the boy's birthday parties. Many birthdays Steve was gone, but I could count on them to help me coordinate and put together a fun party for the kids.

The boys loved spending time with them, they loved swimming in their pool and the cook outs we had.

Aunt Laura would get mad at them for bringing their G.I. Joes into the pool, which often left small boots, guns, and other items stuck in the filter system. I didn't mind her reprimanding them if they needed it. I knew she wouldn't scold them if it wasn't necessary.

To this day Nate and Luke still call them Aunt Laura and Uncle Jay. The boys shared many laughs and great times with them and they truly are family to all of us.

We no longer live near each other, but they've attended both boy's graduations and Nate's graduation from boot camp. I know they'll share in their weddings and be a part of their children's lives someday too.

I'm so grateful for both and their dedication to our boys. Their love has been unconditional and steady in their lives. How blessed we are to have friends like that come into our lives, and yes, become family.

I don't think of them as anything other than our Aunt Laura and Uncle Jay, and will always be thankful to them for being a part of our lives in such a giving, supportive way.

Through our friendship we gave our boys two people that love them as family and that is a gift.

I've heard many times that people are afraid to make friends with a military family because they may have to move, and it will be too hurtful if they become close when it's time to say good bye.

This is so unfortunate. We've met many wonderful people through-out our marriage and moves, and I believe people cross your path for a reason.

Through these friendships you can learn much from others and make wonderful memories. Even if it's for a short time, you'll take something positive away you learned from them and they from you to cherish.

I look back at all the great friends we've made, the great times we've shared, and I'm so thankful for all of them.

Yes, the goodbyes are painful, but you'll have the memories for a lifetime.

Life is about learning, and I know I've learned a lot from the friends I've made in all the places we've lived. It's helped me to cope and navigate many difficult situations. Some things in life are priceless.

Laura and I don't talk every day, but we can pick up the phone and there's no apologies necessary. We know we're both busy, but we make time for each other when we can, and we're a part of each other's lives even though we live far apart.

I know she's there for me and me for her if we need one another. This is such a comfort for me and I hope for her as well.

Some friendships can be draining emotionally. There's not much worse than feeling like you're obligated to be in constant contact or risk feeling guilty. Drama-free friendships are the best.

Our relationship has not been a demanding one, and I believe that's why we're still friends to this day.

It's a gift to have a friendship like that in your life.

If you have even one, you're blessed.

As I'm editing my book, our son Nate has gotten engaged. Laura and Jay will be attending the wedding to celebrate this special day as he begins this new chapter in his life.

When Nate was little we used to say, "Just think, we're going to be planning a wedding one of these days."

Well, here we are, and it came too fast.

CHAPTER 9

RESENTMENT

"Acceptance is not submission; it is acknowledgement
of the facts of a situation, then deciding
what you're going to do about it."
–KATHLEEN CASEY THEISEN

A S A FLIGHT ATTENDANT, I would pack my bags, make sure my bills were paid, take my dog to my parent's house, and head to the airport for my next trip. Even though it was just me, I still had things I had to do before I could even leave to go to work.

Steve on the other hand, would pack his kit bags and backpack, give us a hug and kiss, climb into his truck, and off he went. At times, I'd know about when he would be home and other times I had no idea, and neither did he.

I'd stand at the door holding Luke with Nate running around the house thinking, *how can he just pack a bag and leave?*

I knew the answer but still had the question.

How could he do just that, *pack a bag and leave?*

Because he knew I would take care of everything.

I'd take care of the boys, mow the yard, take care of the dog, take the boys to appointments, and entertain them for days on end with no break or alone time for me.

I had to handle whatever was to happen, as it always did when he was gone.

To top it off, before he would come home (if I knew the date), the refrigerator would be fully stocked with his favorite food, his favorite beer, the house would be clean, the yard mowed, and everything just perfect for his homecoming.

Each time he came home, it literally was like a homecoming. I made sure he could come home to relax and feel missed and special.

I took great pride in how perfect everything looked and hoped he would realize how hard I had worked while he was away.

How could he?

He had no idea how my days had been, but things sure did look good.

I remember when the boys were little, I honestly felt like a walking zombie. I was so exhausted trying to take care of EVERYTHING and the boys too.

The only time I had to myself was when the boys would go to bed. But I was so tired from the day, all I wanted to do was go to bed and sleep because I knew the next day I had to start all over again.

I never had the courage to ask a neighbor, "Hey, could you watch the boys for me for an hour, so I can go get groceries by myself?"

I just couldn't do it. I wish I had. I needed a break but refused to ask for help, and I just figured they were as busy and worn out as I was.

After many of these exhausting times I began to feel resentment. I didn't like the feeling and I knew he was doing what he had to do, but I couldn't control my feelings.

When Steve would come home, I thought, *Oh Thank God, maybe he will take care of the boys and let me have some time to myself.*

Maybe I might be able to go do my errands alone, or maybe go grocery shopping by myself. Then I could actually take my time without having to be in a mad rush or keep two boys within arm's reach.

Unfortunately, this didn't happen often.

He would come home and after the happy homecoming, he would go into the garage for hours at a time, and at the time it was woodworking and drinking.

He would turn up his music, open a beer, and get engrossed in his next woodworking project. Instead of going to the park with the boys and I, or taking us to the beach or wherever, he chose the garage.

Why does he always have to be working on a project when he should be spending time with us?

It was one thing after another. It hurt me, and I couldn't figure out why he would choose woodworking over spending time with me and our two adorable boys who needed their dad's attention.

I'm not saying he didn't spend *any* time with us, he did…to me it just wasn't enough.

I hated he spent so much time away from us, hanging out alone in the garage whenever he was home.

❧

It didn't stop with woodworking. After the woodworking, he started a tree removal business to make extra money. The tree business helped us financially, but really ate up his home time when his business took off.

When he came home from work or got back from a trip, he was on the phone right away, returning customer calls, going out for estimates, or cutting trees and pruning.

These things that took him away from us did make us extra money, and believe me, we needed it — *but it was TIME the boys and I needed.*

I came to resent these jobs he did on the side. Just as with his Navy job, he would get in his truck and leave, leaving me to take care of the boys and do it alone as I had done so many days.

I had these visions of us having picnics, playing ball with the boys, going camping and fishing, or taking a short vacation as a family. We did do a few of those things throughout his career, but not as I had hoped for or needed.

I would think to myself, *why am I alone all the time?*
Even when he is home, I'm alone.

This was frustrating, and it affected our marriage. That's when I felt the resentment creeping in and I hated it.

I couldn't get him to understand the boys and I needed him to engage in our family.

An argument would start if I pushed it too far, and neither one of us wanted to argue in front of the boys, they didn't deserve that.

We moved to Maine for three years for shore duty to spend time together as a family because he had been away so much.

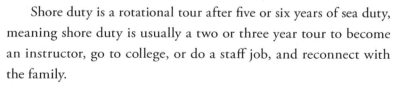

Shore duty is a rotational tour after five or six years of sea duty, meaning shore duty is usually a two or three year tour to become an instructor, go to college, or do a staff job, and reconnect with the family.

What a joke!

When we arrived in Maine, Steve dropped the boys and I and all our belongings off at an apartment until we found a house to rent.

He left us there surrounded by boxes, with a mattress on the floor and was nice enough to put the crib together for Luke. He had to leave for the training facility in the mountains several hours away to start his job as a survival instructor.

He would leave for three to four days at a time, come home and then do tree jobs on his time off.

In between tree jobs he would stink up our rental house by brewing beer in the kitchen and bottling it in the basement.

WHY did he have to always be doing something like this?

WHY can't he spend his free time, the little free time he had, with us?

> *"Sometimes, you need to find the courage inside to let go of the fear, the anger, and the resentment.... the exact things that may be holding you down...and holding you back from the joy of living today."*
>
> —HEATHER STILLUFSEN

When his shore duty tour was over in 1999, we moved back to Virginia Beach and he was assigned to another SEAL Team.

The vicious cycle started all over again.

We hadn't become closer as a family in Maine or spent the much-needed quality time together we should have.

We did live through a bad ice storm with no electricity for six days. I felt like we were living in the pioneer days.

Chop wood for the fireplace, keep the fire going for heat, and cook on our small Coleman stove in the kitchen that got down to 38 degrees.

It was pitch black at 4:00 PM, and hard to keep the boys happy and occupied. It was exhausting.

I'll never forget how excited I was to learn that Applebee's in town had electricity. I took the boys to eat a good meal and was able to wash our hands in warm water without having to heat it on the propane stove.

I do have many wonderful memories of Maine, it was so beautiful there, and in many ways, it reminded me of Minnesota where I grew up. The clear lakes, the four seasons, the small quaint towns, ice skating, sled riding, and the beautiful snow-covered pine trees.

I would load up the boys and try to see as much as we could, packing our lunch and everything they might need for the day, and off we would go on our next adventure. Just the three of us.

We had several family members visit us in Maine, and friends came to visit too. I so enjoyed the company and sharing the beautiful scenery with them, along with the lobster dinners fresh off the boats.

More people came to visit us there than any other state we lived in. We have many great memories from these visits that I cherish.

Maine is also where we found our beloved black lab Moose. I fell in love with him the minute I saw him and so did Steve, once I talked him into going to see him.

He was a big puppy with big paws and really lazy for a pup. Dad was visiting and said, "He looks like a Moose," and the name stuck.

There were blessings in Maine, but there was a lot of pain for me as well. For example, I have a green thumb and love to grow flowers and herbs. I would be planting away and find myself with tears streaming down my face. Or, at the grocery store shopping, I'd suddenly burst into tears for no apparent reason.

Why do I feel so incredibly sad and lonely?

I finally went to see my doctor and found myself with tears running down my face as I told her I didn't know why I was so sad. I explained that I had two healthy boys, a good husband, and that I was healthy, but I had this uncontrollable sadness.

She told me that I was suffering from depression.

Depression? Why would I have depression? Isn't that a mental disorder?

I said, "Well, okay, is there anything I can do about it? I can't go on feeling like this"

There were days that it took everything I had to get out of bed, get dressed, take care of the boys, and in the middle of it all…deal with my crying spells.

Is this what Brian was suffering from when he decided he couldn't go on any longer?

I remember the boys would ask me why I was so sad and I would tell them that I didn't know, but that everything would be okay. My doctor suggested I take an antidepressant that would help with the symptoms.

I was hesitant about this because I was embarrassed that I needed medication and that I wasn't strong enough to fix this myself. So, I reluctantly went to the drugstore and got the prescription filled.

I'm glad I did, because after a period of time, my crying spells stopped, and I didn't feel the heavy weight on my shoulders along with that sense of incredible emptiness and sadness.

I wish I could say that I was only on the medication for a short time and was later fine, but that would be a lie. Depression is a chemical imbalance in your brain and it can be hereditary.

I've struggled with it off and on my entire adult life, and it has been a battle at times, especially when my doctor was trying to get the type of medication and dosage right.

What made it worse at times is that Steve didn't understand it at first, he tended to believe it was the doctor's fault for prescribing meds that caused my mood swings and crying. After he researched depression on his own and learned about serotonin levels in the brain, different medications and how they work, he understood more about it and tried to help me the best he could.

Depression is a much more common topic of discussion now than it was back then. I remember feeling like I had to keep it a secret, because if I told anyone, they might think less of me or treat me differently.

I felt like there was a stigma associated with sharing the fact that I was taking an antidepressant.

 Sometimes we're not equipped to fight certain battles and we need help.

That seems to be something I've learned more than once over the years.

~

When we got back to Virginia Beach, we rented a house for a year while we looked for a house to buy.

Why did we sell our first house in Virginia Beach when we were only going to Maine for three years?

I have no idea. We should have rented it out. That was one of our "not-so-bright" financial decisions.

Nate had gone to kindergarten in Maine and was taught how to write in cursive, but not how to read. Why did they teach this in kindergarten? I had no idea.

We got back to Virginia, and in first grade the kids were reading books, but not Nate. This was only the beginning of school struggles for Nate due to him being so far behind.

My heart ached for him and the struggles he had to go through to get caught up with the other kids. I went to meeting after meeting with his teachers and also learned that if a child is behind, schools will sometimes take advantage of the situation by saying the child has a learning disability when that's not the case.

They do this to get more money from the state for special programs. We had no idea at the time, but many people, including teachers we came to know, later confirmed this was a common practice due to the financial incentives for the school. Hopefully, that practice has changed.

What he really needed was a good tutor and a good teacher that worked together to get him caught up. At the time we were convinced by the staff at school that he had a learning disability.

Only a couple years later, we learned this was completely false, and watched him get good grades, passing his placement tests right alongside his classmates.

I resent that he was made to feel like he was different, or not as smart as his classmates. It had a negative impact on his self-confidence and attitude towards school for years to come.

We bought a house in Chesapeake once our lease was up in Virginia Beach. Steve was gone again, leaving me to move much of our smaller household goods with a Ford Taurus.

I would spend hours driving back and forth between the two houses with the boys and Moose, loading as much as I could fit into my small car.

Aunt Laura came over to help me one day and couldn't believe her eyes when she saw all that I had left to move and pack by myself. Thankfully, she helped me move several loads with Jay's truck.

Without her help, I would've never gotten packed up by myself in time to meet the move-out date. We've since talked about that many times and now laugh about it…but it wasn't so funny back then.

When we lived in Chesapeake, Steve was a Senior Chief, very busy working with strike fighters, running sniper training, and helping his fellow SEAL Chiefs train their Squadron for the war that followed the attacks of 9/11/2001.

After we moved into the Chesapeake house, Steve was still trying to do some tree work on the side, even though his schedule was busier than ever because of 9/11.

We had a detached garage, so he spent many hours out there working on chain saws, ropes, and climbing equipment for his tree business.

He did buy a small boat and the boys were getting older now, so the three of them would go fishing together. It was something that Steve liked to do, wanted to do, and at least the boys could go with him and spend quality time with him.

I didn't know what to do with myself when they went away on these outings. I wasn't used to not having the boys to take care of. I even found cleaning the house enjoyable because I could get it all cleaned up and it would stay that way until they returned. It was the small things in life that made me happy.

Steve's Tree Service was successful for several years, then when we transferred to Hurlburt Field, FL, he decided he didn't want to cut trees in the Florida heat. So, he became a part-time irrigation and outdoor lighting contractor.

I had to fight the feelings of resentment and try to remember why and what made me fall in love with this man.

I would think back to the things he said and the ways he made me feel special, the little things I loved about him, the memories we made together, and the goals we had for our family.

My goal has always been to keep our family together and provide a loving home that our boys would always want to come home to.

"When you come to the end of your rope, tie a knot and hang on."
−FRANKLIN D. ROOSEVELT

CHAPTER 10

MONEY

"Our way is not soft grass, it's a mountain path with lots of rocks. But it goes upwards, forward, toward the sun."

–Dr. Ruth Westheimer

STEVE AND I DIDN'T ARGUE MUCH, but when we did, it was usually about money. I understand why it's a major cause of divorce...we had our worst disagreements over money. Lack of it, to be specific.

When the boys were little we had a housing allowance in addition to his E-5 pay, but we also had a lot of bills. I tried to be careful with spending, but with two small children the money was tight.

I worked odd jobs off and on to bring in extra money, but then I had to pay a baby sitter which really ate into what I made. I always felt like our friends were doing so much better than us financially and I couldn't figure out why we lived paycheck to paycheck. Now, I realize most families are stretched out and many do live that way.

It's expensive to support a family, and it's frustrating when your spouse is in the military, working hard, and gone away so much.

You would think you wouldn't have to worry about money on top of everything else.

Arguing doesn't bring in more money, but I think couples get too stressed over paying the bills, buying groceries, making car payments, and the rent or mortgage.

It's easy to blame one another and that puts a real strain on marriage.

It was especially hard when he was out of town for training, staying in a nice hotel, and he would call to tell me about where they had gone out to eat.

Here I was at home alone with two boys, broke…with no money to go anywhere.

I used to think, *am I supposed to be happy for you that you had a great dinner and we had mac and cheese?*

I know it may sound petty, but it's how I felt. I was used to making my own money when I worked for the airlines and could do and buy what I wanted.

Now, I had very little to spend on the boys or myself, and every dollar seemed to be assigned to a bill.

It was very frustrating for me, I had learned to be independent and now I felt so helpless.

Steve was eventually promoted to Chief and then to Senior Chief, and with each promotion came a pay raise.

Speaking of promotions, when Steve was promoted to Chief, my dad flew in to Virginia Beach so he and I could pin Steve's Chief anchor devices on him at the ceremony.

Steve wanted Dad there because he didn't have a relationship with his dad, and Steve wanted him to share this special day with us.

He had been out of town that week and had just gotten home. During the trip he had been in a big bar brawl in Columbus, GA, with his buddies against a group of Army Rangers and had a bit of a black eye.

Dad and I walked into the ceremony and there stood Steve in his dress khakis, smiling from ear to ear with the remnants of a shiner over one eye.

The only guy in the room with a black eye, my husband.

I think back and laugh to myself, but at the time it was a little embarrassing, especially with Dad there.

Throughout our marriage we have had ups and downs with money. It seemed the minute we got slightly ahead, something would break down or we would have an unexpected expense that would cause us to get behind again.

I remember wishing so badly I could get on an airplane with the boys whenever I wanted to, and go visit my family when Steve was on one of his many trips. I wanted them to see the boys and I wanted the boys to know their family, but the expense of the three of us flying was not in the budget.

We did fly to see my family on Christmas Day when Steve was gone during the Holidays. It was a relief on Christmas Eve to know that Christmas Day we would be in an airport or on an airplane instead of being home alone.

I wish I had put a little money away from each paycheck and let it accumulate for a trip, so the boys and I could have gotten away now and then.

Maybe I just didn't have any extra to put away?

Falling in love and getting married is easy — staying married is tough. Money caused a huge strain on our relationship because neither one of us had learned how to manage it and make it work for us. Marriage is hard enough without money problems and we learned it requires give and take from both of us.

Just recently we signed up for Dave Ramsey's Financial Peace University seminar and learned so much that we didn't know all these years. We've read his books and are working his Total Money Makeover plan. If we had started when we first got married, we would be financially independent right now.

I'm no marriage counselor or expert, but I can tell you that our relationship improved when we stopped blaming each other for our money woes. It makes you bitter towards each other to the point of separation or compromise.

We chose compromise for many reasons, but ultimately it helped us come to agreement on spending, stop blaming each other, and work together.

I think a lot of people these days are accustomed to instant gratification due to the mostly electronic, instant delivery lifestyle we have.

It saddens me when I hear of a short-lived marriage because of money. It seems that some people now feel if their spouse isn't meeting their every need and desire, they can end the relationship and just start a new one.

It's like marriage is disposable, and I feel bad for all the children involved.

Sure, there are many times that Steve hurt my feelings, pissed me off, didn't say or do what I needed him to, but sometimes you have to overlook things, and my goal was to keep my boys with their dad and to keep our family together.

I did make a promise to Steve that if I learned he had cheated on me, I would leave him, and I meant it. I worked too hard, so he could go off and have his career, and there was no way I was going to be mistreated or ashamed by infidelity.

I know many marriages end due to abuse, cheating, or whatever, and I get they must end it, and I understand it.

We all have our beliefs, tolerance levels, and expectations. If you're lucky enough to have a good relationship and love one another, the effort you both put into your marriage will help you through the hard times.

We certainly have had our share of hard times, but I made a vow to love him during the good and the bad, and I had to remind myself of that several times throughout the years.

One of our goals is to own a family cabin on a lake one day. It's a goal we both want and can work towards together. I grew up on a lake and water is healing for me.

I can sit and look at water for hours, whether it's the ocean, a pond, lake, or creek. It relaxes, calms, and gives me peace, and I can really think about things.

Our whole family loves the water, so it's something we all share. I would love to have a cottage my boys could bring their family to and relax and enjoy themselves where we can have quality family time.

When I think about the future, that's one of the things I visualize and hope for. I want our boys to look forward to gathering with us and for all of us to make memories together as a family.

Money can help make a memory, but a memory can also be made with no money at all.

It's memories you leave behind with your family once you're gone.

This year will be our twenty-seventh anniversary. We still have occasional money issues, but things are getting better every year. We're not wealthy by any means, but that's ok.

Our wealth is invested in our two boys. We have two kind, hard-working, and respectful young men that we're honored to call our sons, and that means more to us than any amount of money.

Steve has built a great relationship with both boys and that is due to a lot of effort and work on his part.

I worried that they would never be close due to him being away so much, but he worked on it for years. It didn't happen overnight, but I know he's thankful for the time he invested into their relationships, and is so proud of the men they've become.

I listened to the audio book "Never Broken" by Jewel, and heard her say, "Hardwood grows slowly," and I thought *I love that because it is so true in so many ways.*

Money is important, we must have it to make a living, but invest in your family no matter what your financial situation may be.

The gift of love and your time doesn't cost a penny. My favorite times now are when Steve goes on a hike or walks on the beach with our fur baby Duke and me.

It doesn't cost anything, and I love the uninterrupted time together. We don't have to talk the whole time, but I crave that quality time and enjoying nature.

I tell my boys not to buy me things or stuff, that I just want to spend time with them.

Time is what is important to me.

I look forward to family gatherings far more than what brand of handbag I carry or what designer name I have on my clothes...

those things have never really mattered to me, but time with my family does.

If you have your health, your family, good relationships, and make great memories together, then in my book you are rich.

CHAPTER 11

ROAD TRIP

*"Nobody can go back and start a new beginning, but
anyone can start today and make a new ending."*
—MARIA ROBINSON

WE WERE LIVING IN VIRGINIA BEACH and Steve was at the ten-year mark, halfway through to the twenty years of service required to retire. He was questioning if he should stay in another 10 years or go ahead and get out.

He loved the Teams, but we had gone through so much and it was wearing on us. Luke was six months old and Nate was two...I had my hands full.

Steve took leave, we loaded up our extended cab truck and took off for Montana.

Oh, by the way, as we were loading the truck, his beeper went off and he said, "I have to go in and I may have to deploy, my leave doesn't start until tomorrow."

I stopped loading the truck and thought, *this is just great... all this work packing, and we may not be going anywhere.*

He came home a few hours later and we continued what we had started. I loaded the truck with diapers, formula, bottled water to mix the formula, snacks, and drinks for Nate along with MANY changes of clothes, toys, and two car seats.

Good Lord, I don't know what I was thinking to agree to this?

We drove for days and days it seemed, before seeing all the beauty that Montana has to offer. The beautiful mountains, clear streams, wildflowers, and wildlife eased the stress of the long days driving.

Steve has always loved the outdoors, hunting, and fishing. He thought maybe going to Montana would answer his question about getting out now and possibly moving to Montana or someplace similar.

We would stop here and there and observe the beauty around us. We went to a rodeo which Nate really enjoyed, even at his young age. I remember walking around enjoying the smell of dirt, horses, and leather, thinking, *I might like this life out here in Montana.*

It seemed to be simple and not so stressful. The people were nice and the scenery was beautiful. I envisioned living in a log home, having a vegetable garden, some farm animals, and a horse.

I've always wanted a horse, I pictured myself going for long rides taking in the scenery around me. This life would be good for the boys to experience too.

That night we stayed in a hotel in Bozeman. When Steve was unloading the truck, he met a couple of guys out in the parking lot. He started talking to them and learned they both had been in the military as well, and both were retired.

He asked them how long they served and about the benefits of staying in for twenty years. They both told him he was crazy if he got out now, and he needed to give it another ten at least. They told him about all the benefits of retirement after twenty and he was halfway there already.

The trip was worth it after all. I look back and I really believe we were supposed to go on that trip for Steve to find his answer.

I wanted him to do what he wanted to do. I knew in my heart he would regret leaving the Teams and would be lost without his work family. He loved what he did, he loved who he worked with, he loves the United States, and believed in what he was doing for the sake of our country.

I really couldn't imagine him as anyone other than a Navy SEAL. He lived and breathed it. He wanted to be a SEAL since he was a little boy.

He watched the astronauts on TV when their space capsule landed in the ocean and the Underwater Demolition Team frogmen retrieved them from the water. The Apollo space program sparked an interest in the Navy for him at a young age.

When we arrived back in Virginia Beach, Steve went back to work and I don't think we ever talked about it again.

Be careful what you wish for…you may think you want your husband to get out of the military as soon as possible, *but do you really*?

It scares me to think of what would have happened to him if he had gotten out.

Where would he work?

Could he tolerate the work ethics of people in a normal J-O-B setting?

He had worked so hard to get where he was, would he resent *me* for leaving what he loved?

The military is security, it provides structure, it provides training, and lifelong benefits. I know at times we as spouses dislike the military life, but I must tell you there are many benefits you should weigh carefully.

Today as a retired spouse, I'm grateful for the benefits we still depend on every day.

Because he served until he was eligible for retirement, we have those benefits for good.

I honestly don't know if we would still be together if he had left. I think life would've been too hard trying to make it on our own in the civilian world.

I'm so thankful he stayed in, it was hard and lonely, but we are much better off today, and I'm glad he stuck it out.

After twenty-two years of service, when he did retire, I was right.

My fears were right.

When Steve was on his terminal leave, we moved across the country to Idaho, right next door to Montana. Nate was in seventh grade and Luke was in fifth.

I drove my SUV pulling our camper and Steve drove his truck pulling our boat all the way from Florida to Idaho.

We had not bought a home there, he didn't have a full-time job, he just knew he wanted to live in Idaho to hunt and fish with the boys.

What in the hell were we thinking?

June 28, 2005, was our first night in Coeur d' Alene, Idaho. We stayed in a hotel that had a little kitchenette, living area and a bedroom.

We were literally living out of our suitcases, everything from our house was in storage, as this was our last military-provided move. Our hundred-pound Black Lab, Moose, was in the passenger side of Steve's truck on this journey with us as well.

That night Steve got a phone call from one of his buddies that several of his friends had been killed in action in Afghanistan. Years later, Operation Red Wings would be portrayed in the movie Lone Survivor.

Steve and I just sat and looked at each other, how could this have happened?

So many lives lost from the community at once?

I thought, My *God, the wives, children, parents, brothers, sisters that have lost their loved ones.*

Steve knew several of the men killed that day, they were his friends and brothers.

He was devastated by the news. It was a kick in his gut and I didn't know what to say or do to make it better.

I knew he wanted to return at that very moment and get back into the fight.

We finally bought a home on a beautiful mountain lake after months of living in the hotel and a condo we had rented. We got settled into our dream home and Steve was lost.

He was doing sporadic contract work for a company that trained SWAT teams and military special ops. If he was working with guns and guys in tactical gear, he was happy.

We had no additional salary money coming in on a consistent basis, and I was feeling afraid. We had his monthly retirement check, but it wasn't enough for our family of four to live comfortably on.

He seemed to be going through withdrawal or depression, or maybe both. I knew he missed his job, he missed the Navy, and he missed his teammates.

I think he felt lost and without purpose. He was so used to a structured life and now he didn't have that after twenty-two years.

I found a job to bring in some extra money. I would come home, and he would be sitting at his desk trying to come up with another business he could start on his own.

I know he wished he had stayed in, I know he felt regret for leaving, even though he felt he was doing the best thing for our boys.

The boys were getting into their teenage years then, and he felt he really needed to be there for them. Teenage years are tough and a challenge in any situation.

I'm thankful he was home and there to help me daily, to be a part of their lives, and really get to know them.

But he was not truly happy. I didn't know what to say or do. I felt bad for him because I knew he missed his career.

To be honest, *I missed his career.*

I missed the security and sense of community.

I wasn't used to him being around 24/7 either and that was a big adjustment for me too.

I kept thinking to myself, *surely, he has to go on a trip for a few days.* It had been our life for so long and now he was home every day. I didn't know what that was like and it took some getting used to.

How do you prepare yourself for the day when your spouse leaves the military? Because it will come, and it's not always a happy time.

I'm sure some get out and move on to their next career and are fine, but I also know there are others that become lifers, having their military career in their blood.

It's not so easy for them either to find a career on the outside that meets their expectations, or is as fulfilling as their military job.

The transition to civilian life is a BIG adjustment. It's not easy to watch your husband day after day search for a J-O-B that he can see himself doing for the next twenty years.

He has you and your children (if you have them) to provide for, and that alone is a lot of stress. How can you possibly prepare yourself for such a life-changing event, and at the same time act as if everything is fine?

I've heard some couples don't make it through this stage of their marriage. They made it through a military life, and now the civilian life is just too hard to navigate.

Steve always says, "If I could go back into the Teams today, I would in a second," and I know he would.

He has had four "mini-careers" since then and is finally happy in his current position because he's working with his Navy family again. He's not an active duty Team Guy, but he's as close as he's going to get.

I'm just thankful he's so happy with his job and doing something he really enjoys doing, it took a while to get here, but we did it.

CHAPTER 12

GRATEFUL

"Home is where your story begins."
–A. DANIELSON

WHEN WE LEFT CHESAPEAKE, we moved to Florida where Steve would work his last two years of active duty training SEALs in Close Air Support, working with AC-130 gunships at the Air Force Special Operations Command, Hurlburt Field, FL.

It was a shore duty tour, and at that time in his career we had to decide whether to move to San Diego, Florida or Guam. A couple of years prior, the SEAL Teams had reorganized, which forced the guys into a standard sea and shore duty rotation cycle.

So, after five years at SEAL Team 8, it was time to rotate to another shore duty command. San Diego is beautiful, but we felt it would be too expensive to live there and we already lived paycheck to paycheck.

We felt Guam was too far away and so Florida seemed to be the logical choice. I never had a yearning to live in Florida and I didn't have a good feeling about this move for some reason.

I remember when Steve and I went there to look for a house. While we were eating lunch one day at a local restaurant, I was practically begging him not to move us there. I was having one of my panic attacks and something was telling me not to move here.

We sold our house in Chesapeake "For Sale By Owner" to make the most money we could, and it sold quickly. Once again, the Navy packed us up and off we went to Florida.

Little did we know what was in store for us there. We bought a cute home, enrolled the boys in school and football, and began our new life. We had a pool put in our back yard, the boys loved it and so did we.

We had never had our very own pool before. The boys were having fun playing football. We had friends over for cookouts and the kids would swim. We made some good friends there and our families did a lot of fun things together. Steve would swim with the boys when he got home at night. It was nice.

But wait, there's more!

Within our two years of living there, we were hit hard by Hurricane Ivan and our home flooded twice within a six-day period.

Ivan was devastating to the town of Navarre where we lived. The boys and I evacuated, and Steve insisted on staying behind to take care of the house.

The storm looked so dangerous on the news that Steve left the house as the winds were getting high and joined us in a hotel in Tallahassee. We all sat in the lobby watching the news, seeing the Florida Panhandle get pounded by Ivan.

The reality of just how bad things could get hit me as I talked to some of the rescue people staged at the hotel in preparation for the aftermath.

One of the urban search and rescue gals had a Yellow Lab that was trained as a cadaver dog. I thought, *cadaver dog? Oh my God! You mean they need to bring dogs in to find bodies?*

The seriousness of the storm sunk in real fast and I recalled my bad feeling about moving here in the first place.

As soon as the storm passed, we immediately left Tallahassee. We got on I-10 and headed west towards Ft. Walton Beach, joining a long convoy of utility and bucket trucks, National Guard Humvees, and various rescue crews.

Hurricane Ivan hit the Gulf Coast as a Category 3 hurricane with sustained 120 mile per hour winds. As we drove back into our little town, the destruction was like a movie scene. I had never seen anything like it.

We had no electricity for nine days, no mail, it was hot and humid, and it was downright miserable.

I remember having to weave our Tahoe around giant piles of debris on the main road by our house. There were sailboats, fishing boats, yachts, trees, and pilings, pieces of docks, and decks from oceanfront houses all over the road. There were even several houses that looked broken in half and tilted off their foundations.

I felt so bad for Nate and Luke, it was too much for Steve and I to see and soak in, let alone them at their young age. There was no gas in town, it looked like a war zone, and the grocery store shelves were bare.

I'd call my family with my cell phone plugged into the car charger, but I couldn't describe how bad it really was, there was no way they could understand it unless they saw it with their own eyes.

We were fortunate our house survived intact, the only major damage was to our new fence, which was destroyed, and the pool filled up with red clay muddy water. It took months for the town of Navarre to return to normal.

We had gotten the house put back together and thought the worst was over, but in fact, it was yet to come. The "100 Year Rains" came for a visit the following spring. The water invaded our yard and then the inner perimeter of our home, *the first time.*

I opened the garage door and many of our things were floating... *yes, floating.*

We had no flood insurance because we didn't live in a flood zone, and we didn't flood during Ivan.

The water damage cleanup cost us well over five-thousand dollars. *But wait, there's more!*

I was on my hands and knees scrubbing red silt off our linoleum floor in the kitchen with a tooth brush when the rains started again six days later.

This time the water seeped in from everywhere and there was not a dry spot in our home. The boys were crying and bringing out their bedding to try to soak up the water...*My God, why is this happening to us?*

When the water receded, our carpet and flooring was destroyed and all of it had to be removed. Furniture was damaged, the drywall was wet, and Steve went to work cutting out our carpet and padding to start the drying process as fast as possible.

The cleanup for the second flood cost over ten-thousand dollars by the time we had the house professionally dried and all new flooring installed.

Our pool was under red clay muddy water, yes, the pool was underwater again. This time it took us much longer to get our home back together and to recover mentally and physically.

Before the floods, Steve and I had planned a retirement ceremony and party on base. Unfortunately, this was devastating to us financially, and after twenty-two years of service, a retirement ceremony wasn't going to happen.

I still feel bad he never got to have a formal retirement after all those years of service.

Life just isn't fair sometimes.

It's now a family joke that extreme weather events follow us, as we've experienced some horrific storms just about everywhere we've lived. But we made it through them all, the four of us together, our family.

We sold the house, and it sold quickly even with a recent flood disclosure statement, and we loaded up and moved to Idaho.

We couldn't get out of Florida fast enough.

We had lived through three major life changing weather events. We wanted to move on and forget what we had gone through in our short time there.

We did make some great memories during our tour in Florida. Steve bought a larger boat and took the boys ocean fishing quite often. I would haul the boys to football practice during the week, and thankfully Steve got involved in their football. He went to their games and even helped coach Luke's team.

I loved seeing him out there on the field with Luke and the other boys, and he loved it too. I enjoyed every minute of our family time, I had waited so long for this. I finally started to feel like we were a family, like other families I had watched for so many years.

My resentment was easing up as he spent more time with us. I must add; the reason he was going to retire after his two years there is because *he* realized he had to build relationships with Nate and Luke, and be an active part of their lives.

Nate and he had a strained relationship due to his absence all those years, Steve saw this, and I remember telling him that if he didn't get to know Nate and build a relationship with him soon it was going to be too late.

Nate was much more reserved with Steve, I think it was because he was the oldest, missed his dad when he was gone, and he guarded his feelings.

Luke was always the easy going one and showed such excitement when Steve would come home, I know he missed him too, but he handled his feelings differently.

As you know, two children from the same parents can be so different in so many ways. These things finally sunk in and Steve knew he was making the right decision to leave the job and work family he loved, to be with us—our family—and for that I'm thankful.

The SEAL slated to relieve Steve at Hurlburt had worked closely with Steve at SEAL Team 8. He was also taking the position to spend more time with his wife and children because he too had been away from his family for far too long.

He never got that chance. He was killed in action on Operation Red Wings along with the other SEALS and Army Night Stalkers.

We were given that chance to recover, to try to rebuild our relationship, and for Steve and the boys to really get to know each other.

When I heard what had happened and how many guys were killed in that horrible ambush and firefight, I had to let go of my resentment and feeling sorry for myself for being alone so much.

They were gone because they were protecting our country, and I needed to do everything I had done so he could go and do his job and not worry about what was going on at home. How could he do his job if he had to worry about me and the boys?

I had no idea what the wife of a Navy SEAL would need to do or be when I married him, but through the years I learned, and today I'm grateful I was strong enough to stick it out.

Many don't, and it's sad so many families are dissolved.

It's also heartbreaking to think of the wives that have stuck it out and been the glue for their family only to have her husband go off to war or training and never come home.

Somehow, we made it through the deployments and the absence, the four of us…our family.

I'm one of the lucky wives, I still have my husband.

I used to think, *I didn't sign up for this.*

But I had no idea, no one warned me, no one told me how hard it was going to be, and I knew nothing about the life of a military wife.

I do now, and I have great admiration for all military wives and children.

I'm just thankful we're still a family and the boys didn't have to attend a memorial service for their dad.

I'm also grateful I didn't have to live my life as a widow once again, as I did in my early twenties.

Dear Military Wife,

Please think about the future, life after the military, and what YOU want for your family.

You are strong, and you are the glue that holds your family together. You are the reason your husband can pack his bag and go away for three weeks, six months, or even a year.

You are a mom and a dad to your children much of the time. Your love is why your husband wants to come back home, you give him hope and strength during his weak hours.

He doesn't want to be away from his family either. You are many things to many people and I did not realize this back then and you may not either, but it is true.

Today I am proud of my strength for not giving up on us or our family. I have two amazing sons that know that their mom and dad are here for them, that we are a unit, a family, and that we are a strong family that can get through some hard times if we just stick together.

I don't want to be remembered by my job title at some company.

I want to be remembered as a loving wife and mom. That has been my best job, the job I'm most proud of, and certainly the hardest job I've ever had.

When I look back on how Steve may have not come home from one of his trips, I know how blessed and lucky we truly were and are.

I realize my worst days weren't that bad, and that I had another chance to turn things around the next day. It can be a lonely life, but there's joy and there's happiness, and it's worth the journey and where it may lead you.

One of my favorite quotes is, *"Home is where your story begins,"* by A. Danielson. How fortunate it is that we can write our own story!

CHAPTER 13

MOVING PTSD

"Believe in yourself and your own strength. Yes, things can be difficult, life can be hard at times. You will meet many obstacles along your journey…but know that you CAN and YOU WILL get through each and every one. You have the strength to do so!"

—HEATHER STILLUFSON

I GREW UP IN A FAMILY that moved every two to three years from the time I was eight years old. My dad wasn't military, but a successful sales and marketing manager.

I dreaded every move and remember how hard it was to fit into a new school. I always told myself I would never put my kids through that when I had a family.

From the time the boys were born until Steve retired, we had five addresses. That doesn't sound too bad, but *after* he retired, the number bumped up to thirteen.

After retirement, one of our last moves was when the boys were still in high school. Nate was a Junior and Luke a Freshman. I always felt so bad moving them, but I did my best to get them into the best school we could, even if it meant renting.

I always felt getting them into sports would help them to meet other kids and get involved in the school faster. When they were in grade school it was easier to adapt, but once they got older it became more difficult.

You never want to see your child struggling, feeling they don't fit in, sitting alone in the lunch room. I worried about this every time we moved until I could see they were making friends and feeling more comfortable.

I know we've all had those days they don't want to go to school for this reason or that, and it just breaks a mom's heart. They may or may not tell you why they don't want to go to school, or why they say their stomach hurts.

As a mom, you know there's something going on in school that's making them uncomfortable.

That's when the lioness comes out in all of us moms, and we're bound and determined to find out what's going on and who's doing what to our child.

I'd pray all the way home after dropping them off at their new school, that the first day they would have a good day, and the other kids would welcome them and be nice.

I remember being teased for my Minnesota accent and being the new kid in school…it was so hurtful. My baby teeth were also brown and rotten from a medication my mom had to take while she was pregnant with me.

The kids would tease me and tell me I had rotten teeth, therefore I learned smiling was only for the kids with white teeth.

Kids can be so mean to one another, as I had learned.

I always got involved in the boy's schools they attended. I was room-mom several times, always volunteered to help with Holiday parties, and I made sure the teacher knew I wanted to be involved and would help where I could.

Wherever I worked, I made sure whoever hired me knew that we were a military family, that we had two young boys, and that I was a mom and a dad when Steve was away.

Making that known to my manager or boss at the time of my hiring helped to manage expectations so there weren't problems later if I had to leave work for something unexpected.

The best advice I can give is when moving to a new location is GET INVOLVED. Get involved in school, church, or sports. It will help to pass the time when your spouse is gone and your children's time as well.

We're all busy, but I felt the busier we were, the easier it was on all of us. I also made some great friends in the different places we lived through meeting the other parents in sports.

It always felt so good to go to a practice or a game and see familiar, friendly faces when Steve was away.

Getting your children on a schedule and sticking to it is important.

Steve would come home and want to change our schedule. I had to tell him that he couldn't because our schedule worked for us and it was too difficult to get back on it when he left again.

I know he must have wondered what the big deal was, but it truly was a very big deal to me just to get everything done that I needed to do in a day.

I also tried to make our houses homey for the boys. I would let the boys pick their bedroom paint colors and theme. I wanted their bedroom to be "their room," a room they felt good in and was theirs.

Nate had a military themed room in one of our homes. It had green netting hanging from the ceiling above his bed, camouflage bedding, and he loved to hang his G.I. Joes from the netting. He loved that room and spent hours playing happily with his toys.

Luke always liked more colorful rooms with trucks, trains, and buildings. I now know why; at an early age he was showing his creativity and artistic ability. He's very talented in drawing, welding, creating, and it all began very young.

It just occurred to me that Nate's military room made sense too, as he's now in the Navy.

Both boys were so good growing up, of course they fought and antagonized one another, and that about drove me crazy, but then they would play well together too, most of the time.

I never got a phone call from their school that they had been mean to another child or disrespectful to a teacher, and I was happy for that. I always told them not to make fun of any child that was different than the others or say mean things to other kids and they did well.

Believe me, we had our days, but all-in-all, I'm grateful for how good they really were, and for making my long days a little easier.

Like I've said before, I had to take it ONE day at a time.

I look at Nate and Luke now as adults and I see very well-rounded, adaptable, and respectful young men.

I honestly think the moving helped to create who they are today. It taught them how to communicate with people, and how to acclimate to new surroundings and situations. I also feel they can adapt to new locations and change easily.

They've met many types of people, seen much of the United States, and have really had some great experiences now that I think about it.

I just wish they could have been closer to our families, as we're scattered all over the States and so far away in distance. They never had the big family birthday gatherings, Grandparents at an award program at school, family cheering them on at their sport events, but it is what it is, and we had to live where Steve's career took us.

We all have sacrifices we must make along this road of life.

I always tried to look at each move as a new adventure, a chance to meet new friends, or experience a different state and area.

The boys had the opportunity to experience the pristine ponds, mountains, rivers, moose in the wild, and tidal pools full of starfish at the rocky beaches in Maine.

Every state had unique things for the boys to see and do, like fishing with their dad in the Chesapeake Bay in Virginia, snowboarding in Idaho, or enjoying the beautiful emerald water, white sands, and salt water fishing of Ft. Walton Beach, Florida.

If we had stayed in one location, they may have never experienced those things.

Moving is stressful and hard on everyone, but try to look at the big picture and what you have to look forward to in the area you're moving to.

Try to get excited about the move and your children will get excited too. One thing I learned is when I was unhappy and stressed, my boys usually were too.

They say moving is one of the most stressful things you can do in life, and I feel it's taken years off my life, but we made it once again, intact, as a family.

> *"Continuity gives us roots; change gives us branches, letting us stretch and grow and reach new heights."*
>
> —PAULINE R. KEZER

This morning I once again woke up exhausted and stressed. I have this reoccurring dream that I'm trying to pack up our home and I can't get everything boxed and loaded, and I'm forced to decide what to leave behind.

I know this doesn't sound like any big deal, but in the dream, I'm working so hard and I just can't get done what I need to get done.

I wake up feeling frustrated, so glad it was just a dream, or should I say nightmare?

I told Steve this morning that I had this dream again and how often I have it, and he laughed and said, "Maybe you have Moving PTSD."

Funny as that may sound, I wouldn't doubt it. After all, at the five-year mark in the same house, if we even make it that long, I get very anxious and feel the need to move again.

It's kind of like, "Okay, I'm ready to pack up and move on." A lot of that goes back to my childhood too. I think the longest I've ever lived in one place is six years since I moved from Minnesota at the age of eight.

Each time we move, the last few days as you may know, are the most stressful. We've had several moves where the movers have come in, packed up our home, and delivered the boxes to our next destination. However, since retirement we've also made several moves on our own.

Do-It-Yourself moves in the military are also known as "DITY" moves.

Our DITY moves have been the worst.

The truck is ALWAYS too full, we must leave some things behind, the clock is ticking, and we're still loading.

Just like my reoccurring dream.

Our move from North Carolina back to Virginia Beach two and a half years ago was by far the worst.

We had closed on our home and the new owners were ready to start moving in and Steve was still loading and packing the garage with "his" things I was told "not to pack" when I was packing our 3,000-square foot home, ALONE.

He had already started his new job here in Virginia, and I stayed behind to pack everything up. For one solid month, I worked at packing like I would a job. Eight hours per day I would pack boxes to be put in storage. We didn't have a home to move into at the time.

I had to pack boxes of things we would need for the apartment we would rent while looking for a home to buy. I also packed boxes to take to the consignment shop, purging, but also making a little money at the same time.

Every time we moved, I found more things and "stuff" we didn't really need to move again.

Steve tends to be a procrastinator in his personal life and waits to pack his boxes at the very last minute, refusing to purge any of his things. Then he tells *me* I have too much stuff.

This really aggravates a personality like mine. I start a project and don't stop until its done. I'm a planner with a time frame, and plan each day accordingly to make sure I get the job done.

I think this comes from years of doing everything myself and having to run a household. Our last move was not a happy time in our marriage. I was so frustrated with the lack of planning and the added stress it was causing.

They say opposites attract and I believe this to be true.

We finally got everything loaded several hours after the closing. Once on the road the next day, I thought, *I cannot do this again.* I was exhausted, sore, stressed, and mentally wore out.

Three months later, we were unloading storage units, packing the apartment, and moving into our new home and unpacking, once again.

I must say, living in that bare apartment taught me we really don't need all the "stuff" we've moved time after time. We had just enough cooking essentials to cook meals, our mattress was on the floor, we each brought a suitcase of clothes, towels and toiletries.

The only thing I hung on the wall was our large clock. We did have a kitchen table, loveseat, recliner and our TV. It was nice just having the essentials, we even spent more quality time together.

We could only take the small space of the apartment for so long, so we would take Duke on long hikes, go to brunch, and enjoy happy hour out and about.

I really enjoyed the time we were spending together as a couple, we were still adapting to being "Empty Nesters," and this seemed to ease the pain and loneliness of the boys being gone.

We moved into the apartment just before Thanksgiving and our son Nate was on his first six-month deployment on the other side of world. I waited daily for a phone call or an email, and wondered where he was and what was he doing.

I'd never been separated from my son for six months. As I slowly walked up the dreary steps to our apartment one afternoon with the smell of fried food lingering in the air, I found a box waiting outside the door.

It was an odd-shaped box sent by Nate, and I had no idea what it could be. I opened it and unfolded a beautiful pre-lit crab pot Christmas tree. These trees are popular in North Carolina and I had always wanted one.

I draped a red sheet over a large moving box and set the tree on top of the box so it would be eye level and plugged it in. The tree lit up with white lights and brightened up our little apartment instantly.

I remember I sat staring at the beautiful tree thinking how different this Christmas would be from all our others.

Nate was on deployment, Luke was busy with his life and work, and for the first time ever in all our years together, we weren't in our own home decorated for the holidays.

This year we were renters in a tiny apartment.

I always go all-out decorating, I love Christmas, and I want it to feel magical for Steve and the boys. I want it to be something they remember when I'm gone.

That year in the apartment was much different than all others, it was bare and raw.

As I stared at the tree with memories of Christmas past, tears began to run down my face and my heart hurt.

It hurt for those times our boys were growing up, and the giggles and big smiles as they ran into the living room at the crack of dawn, excited to see what Santa had left them.

I remember feeling so alone at that moment, but this tree gave me comfort. The comfort came from our son Nate thinking of us in this tiny apartment during the holidays and making sure that we had a tree.

Just the thoughtfulness melted my heart and eased the pain I felt.

Nate had no idea after all the years of me trying to make their Christmas special, how special he had just made mine. Christmas was still several weeks away, but every day I woke up, I plugged in our little tree and would sit and look at it and smile. It gave me joy and comfort, which I needed so badly that year.

Another box arrived at our little apartment a few days later, but this box I was expecting. For twenty-six years, my Aunt Syl who lives on a beautiful farm in Minnesota makes sure we receive "The Box" wherever we may be living. The Box always arrives each year before Christmas.

We could always count on The Box to find us.

The boys loved to open The Box on the kitchen floor and unpack all the baked goodies wrapped with love.

Every year is a little different, but kind of the same. Inside are traditional Swedish baked goods, venison sausage for the guys, and hand crafted wooden ornaments Syl makes for the boys.

The ornaments always represent a sport or activity the boys were involved in during that year of their lives. I always tell Syl she could make a killing selling these beautiful ornaments. She also sends me something special she created, and we cherish them all.

When I get out our ornaments to decorate the tree, most of our ornaments are hand made by her. The Box means so much to all of us, she puts great thought into everything in it, and we've come to look forward to the tradition of getting The Box each year.

We closed on our new home a few days before Christmas and we wanted to spend Christmas Eve and Day there. I loaded up our crab pot tree and moved it into our new house. We had very little furniture in the house, but we had that tree.

Steve, Luke, and I enjoyed Christmas around the little tree. Nate was there in spirit, and I felt blessed to have my husband and Luke together with me for that humble Christmas.

For the first time, we opened our gifts from Nate on FaceTime with him from across the world. I felt we were together just to hear his voice and see his face.

We didn't have this when Steve was in the Teams, it would've been so great to see his face during those long times away from one another. It would've been so exciting for the boys to see their dad and to be able to talk to him.

Times have sure changed.

Every now and then, we all need to be reminded what's important in our lives. I learned a lot during that time, and I think of it often.

I remind myself that it's not the *things* in our life, but our family and TIME.

Time to be together and enjoy each other, that is what's most important.

"The best things in life aren't things."
–Art Buchwald

CHAPTER 14

My Team

"True friends are those who really know
you but love you anyway."
—Edna Buchanan

T HROUGHOUT ALL OUR MOVES and this military life, I've been blessed with my "Team" which consists of three women. I hope all women have their own team of special ladies in their life that help them navigate, stay positive, see another side to the situation, lend an ear, and love them through the good and bad times.

If there was one person who was a key part of our lives and was there for the boys and I, it was my best friend Aunt Laura. Since I didn't have any family within a day's drive, it meant so much to me to have Laura nearby. I could always count on her to be there for me, and to participate in our lives.

By being my best friend over the years, she became surrogate family as well.

Even though there is eleven years between my little sister Stephanie and I, we are extremely close. We talk on the phone almost daily, sharing our family lives, making girl talk, and discussing husbands and boys.

Since we are both moms of boys, we have a lot of the same concerns and stories to share with one another. We have a true bond because of our boys, and we embrace it.

I wish so badly that we lived close enough to be able to have family gatherings and sister outings. Unfortunately, there's a lot of miles between Virginia and Texas.

I can call her when I'm sitting in the driveway crying because I'm missing Nate or Luke, or both, and she understands.

We share happy times and laughs, or maybe a laugh or two over happy hour. We also share feelings when we're hurt or angry. It doesn't matter, she's my sister and my best friend.

She loves my boys as if they're her own, and I love her three boys as if they were mine. Sometimes we just know what the other one's going to say, or can pick up the phone and say, "I was just thinking about you." As her older sister, I'm incredibly proud of the awesome wife and mother she is today.

She's been consistent in my boy's lives, they love her, and they know she loves them. She's given me such support and love, and I'm blessed to have her in my life.

We're so much alike, but so different in so many ways. She's a nurse, and I get nauseous at the site of a needle. She's a compassionate, caring person and I know she's a gift to many.

I can't imagine not having her. I'm thankful for her, appreciate her, and love her deeply.

∾

The other Stephanie in my life is my cousin. She's a best friend, confidant, cheer leader, mentor, and the list goes on. I don't know my life without her in it. We grew up together in Minnesota and I could write a book just about us.

We share childhood memories, teenage heartaches, marriage memories, and heartbreaking memories. We now share our empty nest stories, aging woes, recipes, and daily life.

The laughs we share are countless. I can't explain our connection, our love for one another, or our perseverance to stay connected throughout the years.

As a teenager, I remember finding comfort in sitting down and writing her a letter and telling her of what I was going through, or what I was feeling. I always thought she had the best life, and I wanted to be just like her.

Since our family moved a lot, she was my stability, someone constant in my life whom I could trust and count on to always be there.

I remember when she got her first training bra, I thought it was so cool and asked her if I could wear it. She let me, and to me at the time, that was a big deal!

We have so many funny, wonderful memories.

She was my maid of honor when I married Brian, and was there by my side at his funeral. I was maid of honor for her first wedding, a marriage that ended by infidelity which left her devastated.

I was maid of honor at her second marriage and she shared our special day when Steve and I married. We've been there for one another through the good and bad times.

My heart has hurt for her and hers for mine.

I feel grateful and blessed to have this relationship with her, and to be able to say, *we've been lifelong companions.*

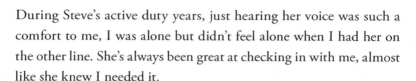

During Steve's active duty years, just hearing her voice was such a comfort to me, I was alone but didn't feel alone when I had her on the other line. She's always been great at checking in with me, almost like she knew I needed it.

I truly feel I've not lived my life one minute without her by my side.

I've needed this relationship and she blessed me with it. We love each other unconditionally, we'll grow old together, this I know.

During our moves when I was feeling down, she would remind me of the good things about moving...meeting new people, seeing new sights, and the adventure of it all.

I used to get kind of mad and think, *she has no idea,* she's lived in the same Minnesota city surrounded by close family her whole life, but she was right.

She's said things to me I didn't want to hear, but really, things I needed to hear from someone I trust.

She knows me better than anyone, and I think we all need someone like this in our lives. It's been such a comfort to me in my life to know she's always there, should I need her.

We all need that one person we can be completely honest, open, and raw with...without having to worry about sugar-coating our words or feelings.

My wish for you is that you have one or several friends and close family in your life that have your back, and go through this life with you and you with them.

I honestly don't know how I would have lived mine without these women.

My story wouldn't be complete without acknowledging and thanking Dad, also known as "Pa-Pa" to our boys. He has given me unconditional love since I was a little girl. He taught me to appreciate nature, to love animals, how to fish and camp out, how to have a sense of humor, and to love country music.

I have called him many, many times throughout my life for advice, desperately needing guidance, someone to listen to me, or to share a happy moment and he always took time to listen to me, no matter the time of day. Knowing that I had him there only a phone call away helped me keep my sanity many times over the years.

I knew that he would always answer the phone, happy to hear my voice and listen to me, not judge me, and offer his calming advice always in the same tone, as my confidant and best friend. He has never pried into our personal lives and always gave his honest opinion when I asked. Sometimes it wasn't what I wanted to hear at the time, but usually he was right, and it was what I needed to hear.

He's been a father to Steve and a loving Grandpa to our boys. Nate couldn't say Grandpa when he was a little guy, but could say Pa-Pa, and since he was the first grandchild, the name stuck. Today, the rest of his grandchildren call him Pa-Pa too. He has been there for all of us unconditionally ever since Steve and I were married.

Traveling all the way from Louisiana or East Texas, he's made it a point to visit us many, many times and be a positive, fun, and loving presence in the boy's lives. Our grown boys love to spend time with him whenever they can see him and we all look forward to any time that we can have with him. We appreciate him, love him, and feel blessed to have him in our lives.

When I was a flight attendant, I was working a flight out of Minneapolis and during boarding in walked my dad, traveling on one of his many business trips. I was so happy to see him, yet shocked, and so proud to introduce him to my fellow crew members. I have always been proud to introduce him to people in my life. I admire him and truly am proud to call him my "Dad". He always told me, "Treat people the way you would want to be treated" and it has served me well.

Once again, I wish that we lived closer so that visits were more often, and more memories could be made. I have many memories from my childhood and throughout my life of him that I replay in my mind. They always bring me comfort and put a smile on my face. Those memories are priceless.

Today, as we all get older I honestly don't know what I'm going to do when I need to talk to him and he is no longer here to answer my call. It hurts my heart and brings tears to my eyes to even think about it. Dad was the first man in my life that I loved with all my heart and loved me back with all his.

I'm thankful for our relationship and the closeness that has always felt like he is there holding my hand, walking through life with me and guiding me, never leaving me alone.

Thank you, Fred A. Danielson, for your unwavering love and support.

CHAPTER 15

WHERE THIS ROAD HAS LED ME

"Never regret a day in your life. Good days give you happiness, bad days give you experience, worst days give you lessons, and the best days give you memories."
—LESSONS TAUGHT BY LIFE

I MARRIED STEVE AND THE NAVY at twenty-seven and I'm now fifty-four. Looking back on the years I've been writing about, it is hard for me to comprehend my daily life back then.

I find myself today longing for the days both boys were at home with us. I miss the noise, the arguing between them, seeing their friends walk through the door, and most of all, being able tell them good night and that I love them.

I was the one who unpacked all the boxes, decorated the house, enrolled the boys in school, signed them up for sports, found new pediatricians and dentists, got acquainted with the area we had moved to, and tried to get the boys excited about their new surroundings.

When both boys left home, I literally felt like I had been left to survive on an island, lost and helpless.

Yes, Steve was there, but what he didn't understand, is that it had been Nate, Luke and I alone for so many years.

Just the three of us navigating through this life.

There was nothing he could say to comfort me.

I just needed space and time to find out for myself how to live each day without my boys, not having that purpose as a full-time mom.

I know many moms are ready for their children to leave and begin their own life, but I wasn't.

I wasn't mentally or emotionally prepared for the lonely days ahead.

I know as parents, our job is to teach our children well, so they have wings to fly. But when both flew out of the nest, I was so very sad to see them go.

Proud they felt confident enough to make it on their own, but I was the one who wasn't prepared for that flight.

They were ready way before I was.

I was working a full-time job when both boys left home, but my head wasn't in my job anymore.

I just waited for one of them to call or text, so I could hear their voice or read a message.

When the boys were in high school, my work schedule at the time had me working every Sunday and Monday, which meant working Mother's Day, Father's Day, Easter, and some major holidays.

This weighed heavily on me as I thought about all the holidays I'd missed with my family, and that I could never get that time back.

It angered me I had allowed a J-O-B to take that time away. I learned from that and will never let a job override time with my family again.

It's an especially bitter feeling if you work somewhere where you feel your work and personal contributions aren't appreciated.

TIME is too precious.

I've told myself I can't live in the past, that I must let it go and move on, but I know better now, and I still have regrets. *#lessonslearned*

As the boys were growing up, we only went on a handful of vacations, it cost money, and it was something we seemed always short of for travel.

The vacations we did have were never extravagant, but that was okay, we were together, the four of us, and quality time was what we needed.

Looking back, I wish we could have taken more family vacations. I feel it's important for your family to get away, relax, and enjoy one another's company, whether it be camping in a tent or staying at a fancy resort.

Steve and I only went away together as a couple a few times, other than that, we went as a family. I have heard how important it is for a couple to get away together alone, but it wasn't always possible.

Money, work, and time off don't always align with the stars to make things easy.

Even if it is a weekly or bi-monthly date night, or an occasional short vacation, it's very important for you and your spouse to get away together and reconnect without the kids when you can.

When the boys were growing up I never had a hobby, I didn't want to spend the money on something for me when the boys needed things and were active in sports.

I wish I had searched and found something I had an interest in, I believe it would have been beneficial for me to do something for myself.

I have always walked or exercised throughout the years, and I would usually use the base gym or join a gym that had day care.

What a relief it was to have an hour or so to myself on those long stretches of Steve being gone.

I've always heard if you take care of your body, it will take care of you. I'm far from the example of a "fit body" but I am blessed I have good health and I feel like I'm in pretty good shape for my age.

Today I take classes at the gym that I enjoy and walk Duke daily. When I walk, I think about things and clear my mind, nature is calming for me. Our son Nate tells me now "Ma, you have to keep moving and exercising at your age."

At your age? I'm not eighty!

It's important that you take care of YOU. We're so busy taking care of everyone else that most of the time we forget about ourselves.

"We must believe that we are gifted for something and that this thing, at whatever cost, must be attained."

—MARIE CURIE

What do I want to be when I grow up?
I still have no idea.

For example, I admire people that say, "I have always known that I wanted to be a nurse." I wish that would've happened to me.

I would love to attain what I'm supposed to *be*.

I just haven't figured it out yet.

I do know this… I know I loved being pregnant. I loved raising our boys, I love being a Mom, and that's what has given me purpose and joy throughout my life.

So maybe I answered my own question.

If I leave this earth tomorrow, I leave knowing I did the very best I could, and I'm extremely proud of the boys we raised.

Maybe I was supposed to write this book and maybe it will help someone during a difficult time, and if that happens then I'll be content and feel I've done something positive for someone else.

Today as I sit here typing, I still wait for a phone call or a text from the boys, I think I always will.

It's getting easier for me, and I realize we raised boys that can take good care of themselves and have strong wings to fly as they continue to impress us.

I'm looking forward to our family expanding and making memories with their families someday.

When our oldest son is on deployment, the worry and fear inside me is still there, and the time away seems to go on forever.

Now I look forward to making his homecomings special.

I send care packages and letters just like I did for Steve, it gives me something I can do for him and I know he appreciates it.

It also gives me a renewed sense of purpose again as his mom.

We live in a large military community and every day I see servicemen and women, and I often look at them and wonder what their life is like.

Is it any easier?

Do they struggle like we did?

Does that wife feel the weight on her shoulders like I did?

I'm sure many things have changed, and yet I'm sure many have not.

I'm reminded every day of the service members that volunteer to protect our country and how they and their families sacrifice so much to support their careers.

I appreciate the military now more than I ever did when Steve was active duty.

I supported him, but I was angry at the Navy for taking him away so often.

Throughout the years of Navy life and especially now that my son is active duty, I have a greater respect and feeling of loyalty to our military, and am much more patriotic than I ever was.

We lived the life and we made it, and for that I'm grateful. I've learned that faith and good health for you and your family is really all that matters.

You can muddle through most problems, but your health is by far one of the most important gifts you can receive.

I see severely injured servicemen and women and I think, *what do I have to complain about today, when every day is a struggle for them to walk or just get around?*

It always puts things into perspective for me and I need that now and then.

When I go through the gate on base I always thank the man or woman in uniform as they check my ID.

I appreciate what they do, and I want them to know it.

I think we forget sometimes to appreciate one another, and remember that we're all in this together.

This road has been long, adventurous, rocky, and yet beautiful. I'm thankful Steve and I have stuck together for this journey, I can't imagine not having him by my side.

Yes, there were times I didn't feel that way, but it was out of anger or whatever obstacle we were trying to overcome at the time.

No marriage is perfect, there are highs and lows, and that's okay. The boys have never said "I'm happy you and dad are still together," but I know they are.

I believe they appreciate the fact that Steve and I were strong enough to keep our little family together.

I hope through us they've learned life is tough sometimes. You must be strong during these times and fight for what you love and believe in.

I'm proud Steve served as a Navy SEAL, even though I had no idea what kind of life I was going to live during his career.

I don't believe you could ever prepare yourself for supporting this lifestyle, *there is no training for this job!*

This job is "learn as you go along," you are literally thrown into it and learn how to survive the best way YOU can.

I've met women my age that are looking forward to their retirement. I won't ever know what it's like to live in the same house and have the same job for twenty or twenty-five years.

I was too busy supporting my husband's career and moving where he needed to go. I did work for a company for four and a half years after Steve retired before we moved here and that was a milestone for me.

Does it bother me? Yes, I'd like to be making a nice salary and say "yes, I've been here for twenty years," but then *would I have had all the other experiences that we've had?*

No.

I can't compare myself to other women. I sometimes look at women that are successful and I feel like I'm a small fish in a fish bowl watching all the other fish swim successfully around.

I know I'm capable of many things, I'm strong, and I'm proud of my family. This has been a long road as I stated earlier, but it was *our journey.*

There was a reason we had to take it and I must believe it was the best one for us. I believe all things happen for a reason. We may not like it at the time but there is a reason.

I've missed out on opportunities in my life, but I've also had opportunities many haven't, and I always remember that.

I don't know the future, but I'm looking forward to growing our family and making those memories that I can replay in my mind that will make me smile and give me comfort.

My goal now is to make traditions for my family, to give my family something to look forward to, and continue to be the glue that's held this family together all these years.

Looking back when Steve and I started dating, we once took a trip to Nashville. I love country music and we went to the taping of an old TV show called Hee-Haw.

When we arrived, Garth Brooks was getting out of a beat-up Chevy truck parked right next to us, with his guitar case in hand, going in to make his first appearance on the show. He sang one of his first songs, "The Dance."

The lyrics are so very true and relevant to my experience in living this life, it's one of my all-time favorite songs.

"If you have a good name, if you are right more often than you are wrong, if your children respect you, if your grandchildren are glad to see you, if your friends can count on you and you can count on them in time of trouble, if you can face your God and say, "I have done my best" then you are a success."

–ANN LANDERS

ABOUT THE AUTHOR

CINDY MESSER—author, mother, and wife of a retired US Navy SEAL, has lived an adult life of strength, courage, and resilience. After being widowed by suicide at only twenty years old, she found unexpected love years later, only to be thrust into a secretive and solitary life as a military wife with no family in the area.

Navigating loneliness, countless moves, and transitions into new communities, her lifestyle has been one of learning to "bounce back." Raising two sons and running a household alone characterized fifteen years of her marriage and taught her how to thrive as a "married-single parent" in the military culture.

While many women spend their lives developing careers and focusing on self-improvement, Cindy continued to navigate change, serving as a military wife and devoting all to her family. The accomplishment she is most proud of is raising her two sons into the men they have become.

Much of her life has consisted of constantly adjusting her sails to keep moving forward, enabling her family to remain intact as she has written about in *Enlisted and Alone*. Cindy is now a Blue Star Mother, with her oldest son on active duty serving honorably as her husband Steve did for twenty-two years.

Residing in Virginia Beach, VA, she now looks forward to making memories with her entire family, including their rescue dog Duke and new grand-puppy Barrett.

Made in the USA
Columbia, SC
25 November 2018